TOUCH TYPING
IN TEN LESSONS

A Home-Study Course with Complete Instructions

in the Fundamentals of Touch Typewriting

and Introducing

the Basic Combinations Method

By

RUTH BEN'ARY

With a Foreword by
DR. HAMDEN L. FORKNER
Professor of Education,
Former Head of Department of Business and Vocational Education,
Teachers College, Columbia University, New York

A PERIGEE BOOK

Perigee Books
Published by
The Berkley Publishing Group
A division of Penguin Putnam Inc.
375 Hudson Street
New York, New York 10014

The Penguin Putnam Inc. World Wide Web site address is
www.penguinputnam.com

Library of Congress Cataloging-in-Publication Data

Ben'Ary, Ruth.
Touch typing in ten lessons.

(The Practical handbook series)
Reprint. Originally published: New York:
Grosset & Dunlap, 1945.
1. Typewriting. I. Title. II. Title: Touch typing
in 10 lessons.
Z49.B47   1989   652,3   88-25477
ISBN 0-399-51529-1 (pbk.)

Printed in the United States of America

50   49   48   47   46

FOREWORD

Typewriting has long since ceased to be the tool of purely the vocational worker. It has more and more become the tool of the professional, the high school and college student, anyone who participates in community activities and everyone who carries on correspondence.

The teaching of typewriting has had many and varied developments. The best methods of presentation depend upon a great many factors, and research has yet to determine which of the many techniques and procedures are best adapted to the great majority of teachers and students. This textbook on typewriting is the outgrowth of experience with specialized groups of boys and girls, men and women. The plan as set forth in this text has had successful tryout with specialized groups at various age and maturity levels. It merits the attention of all typewriting teachers at whatever level and for whatever purpose the skill is being taught. Through experience with this kind of material and this method of presentation, the teaching of typewriting may be advanced materially.

The author has given a great deal of time, thought and devotion to the preparation of materials and plans for their presentation in the hope that teachers of typewriting or students who must learn typewriting without the benefit of formal instruction may find a practical and simple approach to the problem of learning to typewrite. The author does not claim that the materials are entirely and completely new, but she does claim that by following her principles of *Basic Combinations,* and by following the procedures of the text, that the person who wishes to typewrite will find his way greatly smoothed and his learning problems greatly lessened.

The author is to be commended for her pioneer work with special groups and her untiring efforts and unfailing faith in providing for many of her students a satisfying means of earning a livelihood.

The teachers of typewriting and authors of typewriting texts extend to the author their best wishes and hopes for the success of this volume in promoting the learning of typewriting and in exploring ways of teaching typewriting.

HAMDEN L. FORKNER
Professor of Education
Former Head of Department of
Business and Vocational Education,
Teachers College,
Columbia University
New York City, N.Y.

CONTENTS

DEFINITIONS OF THE MAJOR FUNCTIONAL PARTS OF THE TYPEWRITER

1. KEYBOARD: These are the letter keys. When you press a key down, the lower letter or figure on the type key will be written on the paper in the typewriter. For example, when you press the "A" key, a small or lower-case "a" will be written. When you press the key which has "$" at the top and "4" at the bottom, a "4" will be written.

2. SHIFT KEYS: On either side of the machine is a key marked "Shift." To write a capital letter or the figures or signs at the top of the type keys, you press Shift Key with the first (or little) finger of one hand while you strike the desired key with the correct finger of the other hand. Then release the Shift Key.

3. SHIFT LOCK: When pressed down, it locks the Shift Key into position for writing in "all caps" (or all capitals) or for drawing lines across the page. To release

the lock, press the Shift Key which is nearest to the Shift Lock.

4. SPACE BAR: This is the long bar at the front of the keyboard. It is operated with the thumb of either hand and moves the carriage one space without writing on the paper. It is used to space between words, etc.

5. MARGIN STOPS: The sliding indicators (located behind the paper-rest on most typewriters) are moved along to the points on the scale at which left and right-hand margins are desired. When the carriage is moved to either left or right, it then stops at the points on the scale at which Margin Stops have been "set."

6. CYLINDER (or *platen*): The roller of the typewriter, which receives the pressure of the type.

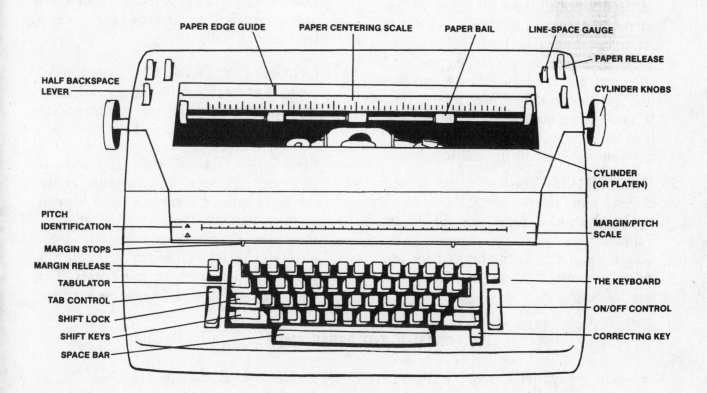

MAJOR FUNCTIONAL PARTS OF TYPEWRITER

7. CYLINDER KNOBS: The knobs at each end of the cylinder, which roll the platen.

8. PAPER RELEASE: A lever at either the right or left side of typewriter which, when moved forward (or, on some typewriters, pushed back) releases the grip of the paper so it can be straightened after insertion into the machine. When carbon packs are used, the release is sometimes opened first to allow easier "feeding" of paper.

9. LINE-SPACE REGULATOR LEVER: A small lever for non-uniform spacing, for writing between the uniform lines, or for exactness in typing on the printed lines of application and other forms.

10. LINE-SPACE GAUGE: This device generally has the figures "1," "2" and "3" opposite or under the lever. When pushed to indicate one of these numbers, it sets the machine for single, double or triple line-spacing, as desired.

11. MARGIN RELEASE: All standard and some portable machines have this device. It is to be found on the keyboard or against the front of the machine. When pressed at either margin, it releases the Margin Stop (for that one operation) in order that type-strokes can be made beyond the margins. It is most frequently used to complete a word or a syllable at the end of a line.

12. TABULATORS: These vary on all machines, and many portables are not equipped with a device for tabulation. Tabulators are used for paragraph indention, for columns of figures and for precision placement of carriage to specific writing points.

13. PAPER BAIL: A rod running the length of the cylinder that holds the top of the paper flat against it. When inserting a fresh sheet of paper, always pull the bail toward you to allow the paper to slip underneath.

14. PAPER EDGE GUIDE: A small piece that protrudes from behind the cylinder, which allows you to guide the paper into the machine straight, and in the same place regularly. This ensures that your margins are the same for more than one sheet of paper.

15. HALF BACKSPACE LEVER: The lever or key moves the carrier one half space to the left. This is used to keep the text balanced when inserting and deleting characters.

16. CORRECTING KEY: A key, usually found to the right of the space bar, used to delete characters. Most electric typewriters now have some memory capacity, and if the character to be deleted is within that memory, the key will delete characters automatically. The correcting key can also be used manually.

17. ON/OFF CONTROL: This is the power switch for the typewriter. In general, none of the functions will operate unless the typewriter has been turned on.

18. MARGIN/PITCH SCALE: The scale is either on the front of the typewriter, above the keyboard, or sometimes it is located on the paper bail. The pitch is the typesize; most new electric typewriters have two, pica (10 characters per inch) and elite (12 characters per inch), or more sizes. The scale for each type size available is given.

CARE OF THE TYPEWRITER

Keep your typewriter covered at all times when not in use. Ordinary dust, accumulated lint, and eraser dust may clog the working parts and interfere with the efficient operation of your machine.

Eraser dust is the worst offender in this

respect. To avoid trouble from this source, do not use the eraser directly over the typebars. Move your carriage to the extreme right or left, so that the point to be erased is over the edge of the machine whenever possible. If the error occurs somewhere along the center of the page, it is usually necessary to press the margin release in order to move the carriage to the desired position for erasing. This procedure is preferable to the habit of rolling the paper up to give enough "clearance" for erasing. Be sure to brush away any eraser dust which falls on the machine.

Brush type faces with a stiff brush. Keep a bottle of good type wash at hand as it dissolves dirt and accumulated ink, and facilitates cleaning. If this special fluid is not available just when you need it, you may use a pin to clean the clogged ink and dirt from letters such as a, e, o, s, b and p.

An occasional drop of fine oil on the tracks on which the carriage travels may be applied with care. It is best, however, to leave the oiling of a machine to a typewriter mechanic. You might do more harm than good as oil can "gum up the works" when not applied properly.

Use a dry cloth for regular dusting of the machine. Never use alcohol to clean the exterior as it is injurious to the finish. A bit of alcohol may be used on a soft, clean cloth and rubbed lightly over the platen (or cylinder) to clean it, but do not use alcohol on any other part of your machine.

Unless the paper you use is very thick, insert two sheets. The under sheet, which acts as a shield in protecting the rubber platen, may be used over and over again. Never permit the typewriter to be used unless a paper is inserted, as striking the bare platen is injurious to the rubber and leaves ink marks which will smudge your paper.

Mechanical adjustments should be left to a repair man.

PRELIMINARY INSTRUCTIONS

CORRECT POSITION AT THE TYPEWRITER

Sit squarely in front of the typewriter. Keep your feet flat on the floor. Table and chair should be of such height that when your fingers rest on the keyboard of the typewriter, your forearms are at slightly less than right angles to the upper arms.

Fingers should be curved in relaxed, comfortable position so that when they rest on the second row of keys (counting from the bottom) they are poised on the four home keys of each hand.

From the beginning, avoid the temptation to place your fingers on the home keys (position) by sight. Locate the home keys by touch. A few minutes of practice will enable you to find the correct position easily and quickly without looking. This is the way it is done:

First, place your hands on your lap. Then

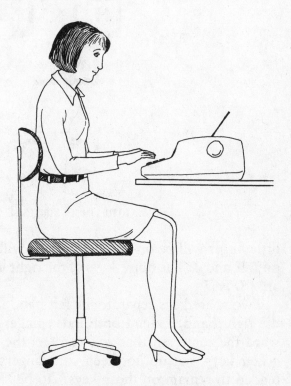

CORRECT POSITION AT THE TYPEWRITER

raise them slowly so that the backs of your finger tips touch the front base of the typewriter. Let your finger tips creep lightly over the base until they barely touch the space bar.

Pass lightly over the space bar without pressing it down, and let your fingers come to rest on the bottom row of keys. From this row, move slowly up to the second row. Stay there.

With the little finger of your left hand feel outward and make sure it is resting on the end key of the second row. That key is the letter A. If your fingers are not spread apart the others rest naturally on S D and F. The home keys of the left hand are A S D F.

The little finger of your right hand should be on the *second* key from the right end of the same row. Feel outward and make sure there is a key to spare on the right. If there is, your

Now put your hands back in your lap and start over again, practicing this method of finding position until you can locate the home keys easily by touch. Repeat these thoughts in your mind with each attempt as your hands go through the motions:

Over the space bar, over the first row, onto the second row. End key on the left side. Second key on the right side (feel outward for the spare key). Feel only two spare keys in the middle, but DO NOT KEEP the index fingers extended.

As soon as you have learned to locate position by touch you are ready to proceed with the first lesson. Keep your hands in position at all times. If your hands shift around the keyboard and go off position you will make errors.

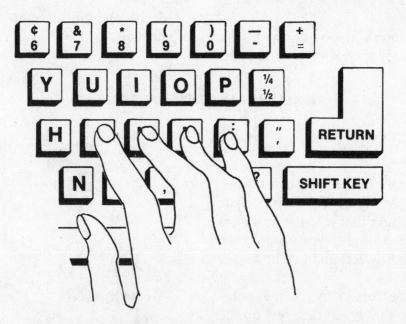

LITTLE FINGER STRIKES SEMICOLON; OTHER FINGERS ON L, K, AND J

little finger will be on ; and the others will fall on L K and J. The home keys of the right hand are ; L K J .

Two spare keys separate the left hand from the right hand. Extend both index fingers toward the center so that you can feel the two center keys, but do not keep your fingers extended to remain on those keys. Do NOT try to memorize the center keys by sight.

When striking a key, it is not necessary to remove all of the other fingers from the keys in order to make the stroke. Do not, however, bear down on the home keys. Strokes should be staccato—sharp and quick. Strike each key so that your finger seems to bounce with each stroke. Do not hang onto it.

The thumbs are used only on the space bar. Most typists prefer to strike the space bar with the thumb of the *right* hand. Should your left thumb have greater flexibility, use that one to operate the space bar. Do not space with both thumbs at once.

Adjust the typewriter for single line spacing, and the margin stops for an inch margin on each side—unless otherwise instructed.

Use standard-size typewriting paper—8½ x 11 inches.

LESSON ONE

BASIC HORIZONTAL COMBINATIONS

Follow these instructions as though they were being dictated. Italics indicate the voice and typewritten letters indicate the strokes with which you follow through.

LEFT HAND   EXERCISE 1.

With the little finger of the left hand, strike a. *With the next finger, strike* s. *With the next, strike* d. *With the next, strike* f. *Now extend the "f" finger to the spare key next to it, and strike* g. *Do not keep your finger on the "g" but let it slip back to home key "f." Space once* *with your right thumb. KEEP YOUR FINGERS ON THE KEYS.*

What you have typed should appear like this: asdfg.

Repeat this combination of letters across an entire line, memorizing it as you read the "dictation" and strokes aloud thus:

asdfg *space* asdfg *space* asdfg

Type another line of this combination with quick even strokes, properly spaced so that your paper has two lines like the following:

asdfg asdfg asdfg asdfg asdfg asdfg asdfg asdfg
asdfg asdfg asdfg asdfg asdfg asdfg asdfg asdfg

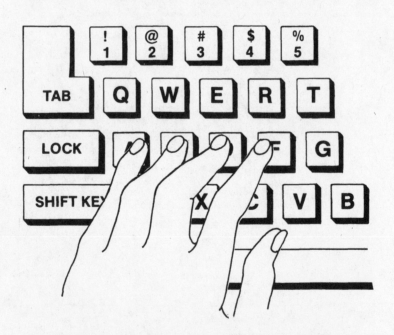

LITTLE FINGER STRIKES A; OTHER FINGERS ON S, D, AND F

Now, without striking the keys or looking at the text (to which we will hereafter refer as "copy") or at your paper, say this combination over and over to yourself until you are able to rattle it off from memory. When you know it thoroughly, you are ready for the right hand strokes. Remember, however, to keep both hands in position even though you may be practicing the strokes of only one hand.

Skip a line before starting another exercise so that you will have double line-spaces between groups. Try to keep exercises neatly blocked like the two lines of Exercise 1.

LITTLE FINGER STRIKES A;

NEXT FINGER STRIKES S;

NEXT FINGER STRIKES D;

INDEX FINGER STRIKES F AND G.

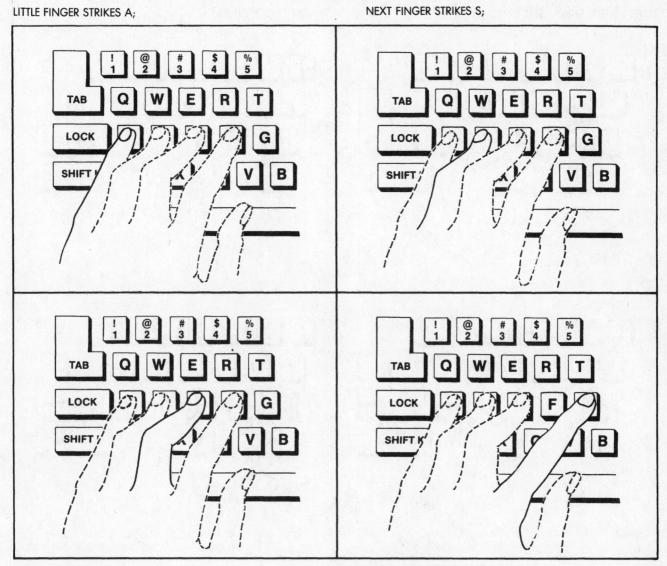

RIGHT HAND   EXERCISE 2.

(For the sake of rhythm we will call the semi-colon (;) "semi.")

With the little finger of the right hand, strike ;. With the next finger, strike l. With the next, strike k. With the next, strike j. Now extend the "j" finger to the spare key next to it, and strike h. Do not keep your finger on the "b" but let it slip back to home key "j." Space once with your left thumb. KEEP YOUR FINGERS ON THE KEYS.

;lkjh ;lkjh ;lkjh ;lkjh ;lkjh ;lkjh ;lkjh ;lkjh
;lkjh ;lkjh ;lkjh ;lkjh ;lkjh ;lkjh ;lkjh ;lkjh

What you have typed should appear like this: ;lkjh.

Repeat this combination of letters across an entire line, memorizing it as you read the dictation aloud, thus:

;lkjh *space* ;lkjh *space* ;lkjh

Type another line of this combination with quick even strokes, properly spaced so that you have:

LITTLE FINGER STRIKES SEMICOLON;

NEXT FINGER STRIKES L;

NEXT FINGER STRIKES K;

INDEX FINGER STRIKES J AND H.

ALTERNATING HANDS   EXERCISE 3.

When you have memorized the above combination, you are ready to alternate—first left, then right hand, saying:

asdfg *space* ;lkjh *space* asdfg

Again, without looking at copy or your paper, memorize the two combinations so that you can rattle them off alternately as they appear in the two lines just typed.

Repeat across the line, memorizing as you go along:

asdfg ;lkjh asdfg ;lkjh asdfg ;lkjh asdfg ;lkjh
asdfg ;lkjh asdfg ;lkjh asdfg ;lkjh asdfg ;lkjh

The two combinations you have learned are the *Basic Horizontal Combinations*. When you can say them repeatedly without hesitation, you may go on with Exercise 4.

HORIZONTAL COMBINATIONS

EXERCISE 4.

In this exercise we scramble the dictation of letters of both combinations. Do not even "steal a glance" at your paper this time. *And do not read ahead in the text.* Keep your eyes on the copy and follow the dictation, stroke for stroke, and space for space, until the text instructs you to "look at what you have written." Do not strike carelessly without thinking. If you are hesitant about a letter, think the two combinations through your mind before making the stroke. If necessary, repeat "asdfg ;lkjh"

to yourself before every actual stroke. Space *only* when the word "space" appears in this "dictated matter." Be sure you have a double line-space between the previous exercise and this one. Be sure your position is correct.

a *space* lad *space* has *space* a *space* glad *space* dad; *space* dad *space* had *space* half *space* a *space* shad *space* salad;

Now look at what you have written. Your line should read:

a lad has a glad dad; dad had half a shad salad;

If you have followed the text carefully, you have typed not only words, but phrases, entirely by touch—and in your first hour of instruction! Of course, writing these phrases "by touch" for the first time was slower than you could have done "by sight." However, familiarity with the keys is entirely a matter of practice and repetition.

Now type five lines of the two phrases above. By the time you have typed your fifth line, you will find that your speed in writing that line has increased considerably through the repetition practice.

a lad has a glad dad; dad had half a shad salad;
a lad has a glad dad; dad had half a shad salad;
a lad has a glad dad; dad had half a shad salad;
a lad has a glad dad; dad had half a shad salad;
a lad has a glad dad; dad had half a shad salad;

For supplementary practice, drill yourself in the following words formed by the letters of the *Basic Horizontal Combinations*—asdfg and ;lkjh.

ask jag gas lag fad half lash gash lass glass
ash sag gag hag had sash fall hash dash slash

PRACTICE MODEL

Lesson 1

```
asdfg ;lkjh asdfg ;lkjh asdfg ;lkjh asdfg ;lkjh asdfg ;lkjh
asdfg ;lkjh asdfg ;lkjh asdfg ;lkjh asdfg ;lkjh asdfg ;lkjh
asdfg ;lkjh asdfg ;lkjh asdfg ;lkjh asdfg ;lkjh asdfg ;lkjh
asdfg ;lkjh asdfg ;lkjh asdfg ;lkjh asdfg ;lkjh asdfg ;lkjh
asdfg ;lkjh asdfg ;lkjh asdfg ;lkjh asdfg ;lkjh asdfg ;lkjh


a lad has a glad dad; dad had half a shad salad;
a lad has a glad dad; dad had half a shad salad;
a lad has a glad dad; dad had half a shad salad;
a lad has a glad dad; dad had half a shad salad;
a lad has a glad dad; dad had half a shad salad;


ask jag gas lag fad half lash gash lass glass
ask jag gas lag fad half lash gash lass glass
ask jag gas lag fad half lash gash lass glass
ask jag gas lag fad half lash gash lass glass
ask jag gas lag fad half lash gash lass glass


ash sag gag hag had sash fall hash dash slash
ash sag gag hag had sash fall hash dash slash
ash sag gag hag had sash fall hash dash slash
ash sag gag hag had sash fall hash dash slash
ash sag gag hag had sash fall hash dash slash


dad has a gag; a lass has a sash; a lad has a lash as a fad;
dad has a gag; a lass has a sash; a lad has a lash as a fad;
dad has a gag; a lass has a sash; a lad has a lash as a fad;
dad has a gag; a lass has a sash; a lad has a lash as a fad;
dad has a gag; a lass has a sash; a lad has a lash as a fad;
```

LESSON TWO

BASIC DIAGONAL COMBINATIONS

Keeping eyes off the keys, locate proper position by touch. Type two lines of the *Basic Horizontal Combinations,* alternating left and right hand, properly spaced. Say them aloud as you go along.

```
asdfg ;lkjh asdfg ;lkjh asdfg ;lkjh asdfg ;lkjh
asdfg ;lkjh asdfg ;lkjh asdfg ;lkjh asdfg ;lkjh
```

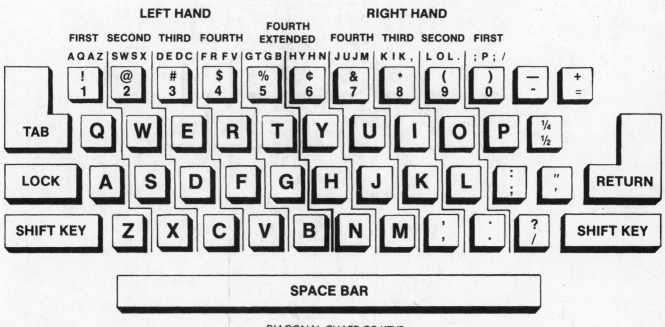

DIAGONAL CHART OF KEYS

If you know these combinations thoroughly, you are ready to start on the *Basic Diagonal Combinations,* which include all the letters of the keyboard and certain marks of punctuation.

Below you will find a keyboard chart of the *Basic Diagonal Combinations.* At this point, study the chart for a minute. Notice the diagonal slant of the keys. Each finger strikes within its diagonal line, with the exception of the index finger which extends to operate within two diagonal lines.

Ordinarily we think of the index finger as the first finger, and the little finger as the fourth. In learning the keyboard by the *Basic Combinations Method,* however, you will find it easier to think of your fingers in the reverse order.

Each hand has five *Basic Diagonal Combinations.* The little finger strikes the "first" finger combination, the next one strikes the "second," the middle finger controls the "third," while the index finger controls the "fourth" and the "fourth *extended*" combinations.

LEFT HAND   EXERCISE 1.

Follow the method of dictation and stroke used in Lesson One.

"First" Finger

Strike a. *With the same finger, reach up and slightly to the outward edge to strike* q. *Let your finger slip back to position to strike again the letter* a. *From "a" reach down and slightly inward to strike* z, *then space.*

That completes the first diagonal combination, and the little finger goes back to rest on "a." On your paper you should have: aqaz.

Type the aqaz-combination across the line, repeating these directions as you go through the motions:

aqaz aqaz aqaz aqaz aqaz aqaz aqaz aqaz aqaz aqaz aqaz aqaz
aqaz aqaz aqaz aqaz aqaz aqaz aqaz aqaz aqaz aqaz aqaz aqaz

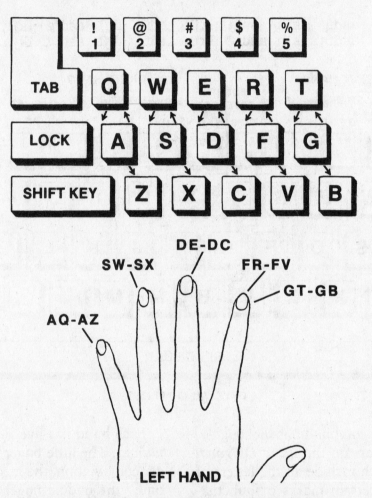

ACTION OF LEFT HAND STRIKING KEYS

Small finger on A, then Q, then A, then Z
Next finger on S, then W, then S, then X
Next finger on D, then E, then D, then C
Index finger on F, then R, then F, then V
Index finger on G, then T, then G, then B

After you have completed two lines of the first combination, proceed with the second, bearing in mind the same diagonal direction.

"Second" Finger

s. *Up and out for* **w.** *Back to* **s.** *Down and in for* **x.** *Space.*

Type the **swsx**-combination across two lines.

```
swsx swsx swsx swsx swsx swsx swsx swsx swsx swsx swsx swsx swsx
swsx swsx swsx swsx swsx swsx swsx swsx swsx swsx swsx swsx swsx
```

Now close your eyes and recite the first two *Diagonal Combinations* before proceeding with the third.

"Third" Finger

d. *Up and out for* e. *Back to* d. *Down and in for* c. *Space.*

Type the **dedc**-combination across two lines.

```
dedc dedc dedc dedc dedc dedc dedc dedc dedc dedc dedc dedc dedc
dedc dedc dedc dedc dedc dedc dedc dedc dedc dedc dedc dedc dedc
```

Now close your eyes and recite the first three *Diagonal Combinations* before proceeding with the fourth.

"Fourth" Finger

f. *Up and out for* r. *Back to* f. *Down and in for* v. *Space.*

Type the **frfv**-combination across five lines.

```
frfv frfv frfv frfv frfv frfv frfv frfv frfv frfv frfv frfv frfv
frfv frfv frfv frfv frfv frfv frfv frfv frfv frfv frfv frfv frfv
frfv frfv frfv frfv frfv frfv frfv frfv frfv frfv frfv frfv frfv
frfv frfv frfv frfv frfv frfv frfv frfv frfv frfv frfv frfv frfv
frfv frfv frfv frfv frfv frfv frfv frfv frfv frfv frfv frfv frfv
```

Recite the four combinations, before proceeding with the fifth.

"Fourth Extended" Finger

For the fourth-extended combination of the left hand you have a long reach for each stroke. Keeping the first three fingers on A S and D, extend the index finger for each stroke of the **gtgb**-combination, as follows:

g. *Up and out for* t. *Back to* g. *Down and in for* b. *Space.*

Type the **gtgb**-*combination across five lines.*

```
gtgb gtgb gtgb gtgb gtgb gtgb gtgb gtgb gtgb gtgb gtgb gtgb gtgb
gtgb gtgb gtgb gtgb gtgb gtgb gtgb gtgb gtgb gtgb gtgb gtgb gtgb
gtgb gtgb gtgb gtgb gtgb gtgb gtgb gtgb gtgb gtgb gtgb gtgb gtgb
gtgb gtgb gtgb gtgb gtgb gtgb gtgb gtgb gtgb gtgb gtgb gtgb gtgb
gtgb gtgb gtgb gtgb gtgb gtgb gtgb gtgb gtgb gtgb gtgb gtgb gtgb
```

Recite the five *Basic Diagonal Combinations* of the left hand.
Repeat all of Exercise 1 thus:

```
aqaz aqaz aqaz aqaz aqaz aqaz aqaz aqaz aqaz
swsx swsx swsx swsx swsx swsx swsx swsx swsx
dedc dedc dedc dedc dedc dedc dedc dedc dedc
frfv frfv frfv frfv frfv frfv frfv frfv frfv
gtgb gtgb gtgb gtgb gtgb gtgb gtgb gtgb gtgb
```

Skip a line and type two lines of the left hand *Diagonal Combinations* in their order, thus:

```
aqaz swsx dedc frfv gtgb aqaz swsx dedc frfv gtgb
aqaz swsx dedc frfv gtgb aqaz swsx dedc frfv gtgb
```

Before attempting Exercise 2, you should be able to recite these five combinations without hesitation.

With the left hand, the combination direction was "up and *out,* down and *in.*" With the right hand, however, the stroke is "up and *in,* down and *out*" (this direction being in its relation to the right edge of the machine).

RIGHT HAND   EXERCISE 2.

Strike semi ;. *With the same finger reach up and slightly inward to strike* p. *Let your finger slip back to position to strike the semi again* ; *then reach down and outward to strike* / *then space.* (This oblique line which you have just struck will be referred to as "diagonal." Its uses will be discussed in Lesson Five.)

In dictating this combination, the voice says, *"Semi p semi diagonal."* Bear in mind the "up and in, down and out" direction as you type it across the line. Recite the ;p;/-combination as you type it across the line.

```
;p;/ ;p;/ ;p;/ ;p;/ ;p;/ ;p;/ ;p;/ ;p;/ ;p;/ ;p;/ ;p;/ ;p;/ ;p;/
;p;/ ;p;/ ;p;/ ;p;/ ;p;/ ;p;/ ;p;/ ;p;/ ;p;/ ;p;/ ;p;/ ;p;/ ;p;/
```

After you have completed two lines of the first combination, proceed with the second, bearing in mind the same diagonal direction.

"Second" Finger

1. *Up and in for* o. *Back to* 1. *Down and out for* . *Space.*

Type the lol.-combination across the line as you dictate:

```
lol. lol. lol. lol. lol. lol. lol. lol. lol. lol. lol. lol. lol.
lol. lol. lol. lol. lol. lol. lol. lol. lol. lol. lol. lol. lol.
```

Close your eyes and recite combinations one and two for the right hand.

"Third" Finger

k. *Up and in for* i. *Back to* k. *Down and out for* ,. *Space.*

Type the kik,-combination across the line, remembering the directions:

```
kik, kik, kik, kik, kik, kik, kik, kik, kik, kik, kik, kik, kik,
kik, kik, kik, kik, kik, kik, kik, kik, kik, kik, kik, kik, kik,
```

Now close your eyes and recite the three combinations for the right hand without looking at the keyboard or paper.

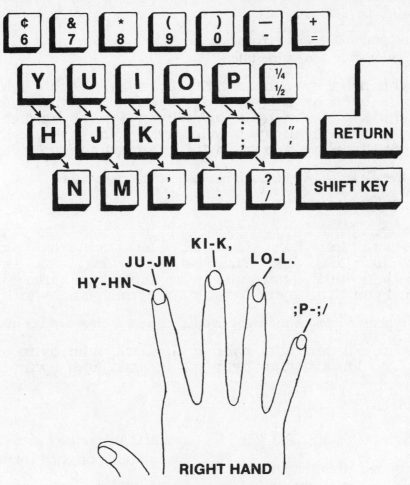

ACTION OF RIGHT HAND STRIKING KEYS

Small finger on ;, then P,, then ;, then /
Next finger on L, then O, then L, then .
Next finger on K, then I, then K, then ,
Index finger on J, then U, then J, then M
Index finger on H, then Y, then H, then N

"Fourth" Finger

j. *Up and in for* u. *Back to* j. *Down and out for* m. *Space.*

Type the jujm-combination across the line as you dictate.

```
jujm  jujm  jujm  jujm  jujm  jujm  jujm  jujm  jujm  jujm  jujm  jujm  jujm
jujm  jujm  jujm  jujm  jujm  jujm  jujm  jujm  jujm  jujm  jujm  jujm  jujm
jujm  jujm  jujm  jujm  jujm  jujm  jujm  jujm  jujm  jujm  jujm  jujm  jujm
jujm  jujm  jujm  jujm  jujm  jujm  jujm  jujm  jujm  jujm  jujm  jujm  jujm
jujm  jujm  jujm  jujm  jujm  jujm  jujm  jujm  jujm  jujm  jujm  jujm  jujm
```

Close your eyes and recite the first four combinations for the right hand.

"Fourth Extended" Finger

For the fourth-extended combination of the right hand, you have a long reach for each stroke. Keeping the first three fingers of this hand on ; L K , extend the index finger for each stroke of the hyhn-combination, and type the fourth-extended combination across the line:

```
hyhn hyhn hyhn hyhn hyhn hyhn hyhn hyhn hyhn hyhn hyhn hyhn hyhn
hyhn hyhn hyhn hyhn hyhn hyhn hyhn hyhn hyhn hyhn hyhn hyhn hyhn
hyhn hyhn hyhn hyhn hyhn hyhn hyhn hyhn hyhn hyhn hyhn hyhn hyhn
hyhn hyhn hyhn hyhn hyhn hyhn hyhn hyhn hyhn hyhn hyhn hyhn hyhn
hyhn hyhn hyhn hyhn hyhn hyhn hyhn hyhn hyhn hyhn hyhn hyhn hyhn
```

Now recite the five *Basic Diagonal Combinations* of the right hand.

Repeat Exercise 2 thus:

```
;p;/    ;p;/    ;p;/    ;p;/    ;p;/    ;p;/    ;p;/    ;p;/    ;p;/    ;p;/
lol.    lol.    lol.    lol.    lol.    lol.    lol.    lol.    lol.    lol.
kik,    kik,    kik,    kik,    kik,    kik,    kik,    kik,    kik,    kik,
jujm    jujm    jujm    jujm    jujm    jujm    jujm    jujm    jujm    jujm
hyhn    hyhn    hyhn    hyhn    hyhn    hyhn    hyhn    hyhn    hyhn    hyhn
```

Skip a line and type two lines of the right hand *Diagonal Combinations* in their order, thus:

```
;p;/ lol. kik, jujm hyhn ;p;/ lol. kik, jujm hyhn
;p;/ lol. kik, jujm hyhn ;p;/ lol. kik, jujm hyhn
```

DIAGONAL COMBINATIONS   EXERCISE 3.

You have now covered all the letters of the keyboard. Type five lines of all the *Basic Di-agonal Combinations* in the following manner, concentrating on each combination as you go along:

```
aqaz swsx dedc frfv gtgb ;p;/ lol. kik, jujm hyhn
aqaz swsx dedc frfv gtgb ;p;/ lol. kik, jujm hyhn
aqaz swsx dedc frfv gtgb ;p;/ lol. kik, jujm hyhn
aqaz swsx dedc frfv gtgb ;p;/ lol. kik, jujm hyhn
aqaz swsx dedc frfv gtgb ;p;/ lol. kik, jujm hyhn
```

Before proceeding with the next lesson you should be able to recite without hesitation the two *Basic Horizontal Combinations* and the ten *Basic Diagonal Combinations* in the order in which they were learned:

```
asdfg ;lkjh
aqaz swsx dedc frfv gtgb ;p;/ lol. kik, jujm hyhn
```

Let these combinations haunt you throughout the remainder of the day and evening. Notice the strange little "words" some of these combinations appear to be. Visualize them. Repeat them as though you were saying your prayers before you go to sleep tonight, *thinking into each finger in proper order* as you go along. Repeat them again in the morning.

PRACTICE MODEL

Lesson 2

```
asdfg ;lkjh asdfg ;lkjh asdfg ;lkjh asdfg ;lkjh asdfg ;lkjh
asdfg ;lkjh asdfg ;lkjh asdfg ;lkjh asdfg ;lkjh asdfg ;lkjh
asdfg ;lkjh asdfg ;lkjh asdfg ;lkjh asdfg ;lkjh asdfg ;lkjh
asdfg ;lkjh asdfg ;lkjh asdfg ;lkjh asdfg ;lkjh asdfg ;lkjh
asdfg ;lkjh asdfg ;lkjh asdfg ;lkjh asdfg ;lkjh asdfg ;lkjh
```

```
a lad has a glad dad; dad had half a shad salad;
a lad has a glad dad; dad had half a shad salad;
a lad has a glad dad; dad had half a shad salad;
a lad has a glad dad; dad had half a shad salad;
a lad has a glad dad; dad had half a shad salad;
```

```
dad has a gag; dad has a gag; dad has a gag; dad has a gag;
dad has a gag; dad has a gag; dad has a gag; dad has a gag;
dad has a gag; dad has a gag; dad has a gag; dad has a gag;
dad has a gag; dad has a gag; dad has a gag; dad has a gag;
dad has a gag; dad has a gag; dad has a gag; dad has a gag;
```

```
a lass has a sash; a lass has a sash; a lass has a sash;
a lass has a sash; a lass has a sash; a lass has a sash;
a lass has a sash; a lass has a sash; a lass has a sash;
a lass has a sash; a lass has a sash; a lass has a sash;
a lass has a sash; a lass has a sash; a lass has a sash;
```

```
a lad has a lash as a fad; a lad has a lash as a fad;
a lad has a lash as a fad; a lad has a lash as a fad;
a lad has a lash as a fad; a lad has a lash as a fad;
a lad has a lash as a fad; a lad has a lash as a fad;
a lad has a lash as a fad; a lad has a lash as a fad;
```

```
hag hag hag hag hag hag hag hag hag hag hag hag hag hag hag
hag hag hag hag hag hag hag hag hag hag hag hag hag hag hag
hag hag hag hag hag hag hag hag hag hag hag hag hag hag hag
hag hag hag hag hag hag hag hag hag hag hag hag hag hag hag
hag hag hag hag hag hag hag hag hag hag hag hag hag hag hag
```

```
ask ask ask ask ask ask ask ask ask ask ask ask ask ask ask
ask ask ask ask ask ask ask ask ask ask ask ask ask ask ask
ask ask ask ask ask ask ask ask ask ask ask ask ask ask ask
ask ask ask ask ask ask ask ask ask ask ask ask ask ask ask
ask ask ask ask ask ask ask ask ask ask ask ask ask ask ask
```

```
aqaz swsx dedc frfv gtgb ;p;/ lol. kik, jujm hyhn
aqaz swsx dedc frfv gtgb ;p;/ lol. kik, jujm hyhn
aqaz swsx dedc frfv gtgb ;p;/ lol. kik, jujm hyhn
aqaz swsx dedc frfv gtgb ;p;/ lol. kik, jujm hyhn
aqaz swsx dedc frfv gtgb ;p;/ lol. kik, jujm hyhn
```

LESSON THREE

TYPING THE ALPHABET

Review Drill

Type two lines of the *Basic Horizontal Combinations.*

```
asdfg ;lkjh asdfg ;lkjh asdfg ;lkjh asdfg ;lkjh
asdfg ;lkjh asdfg ;lkjh asdfg ;lkjh asdfg ;lkjh
```

Skip a line and type two lines of the *Basic Diagonal Combinations.*

```
aqaz swsx dedc frfv gtgb ;p;/ lol. kik, jujm hyhn
aqaz swsx dedc frfv gtgb ;p;/ lol. kik, jujm hyhn
```

Can you recite all the *Basic Combinations* in their proper order without hesitating? If so, you are ready to type them in alphabetical order.

The alphabet will be given in three parts. The first part is composed of left hand strokes; the second part is composed of right hand strokes; the third section requires left and right hand strokes.

LEFT HAND   EXERCISE 1.

Strike a. *Now, long reach to* b *of the* gtgb-*combination. On the lower row again, strike* c *of the* dedc-*combination. Up the ladder of the same Diagonal Combination for* d *and* e. *Now* f *and* g. *Space.* You should now have abcdefg.

Practice at least five lines of this group across the page, saying: a. *Long reach* b. *Up the ladder* c d e. *Then* f g.

```
abcdefg abcdefg abcdefg abcdefg abcdefg abcdefg abcdefg abcdefg
abcdefg abcdefg abcdefg abcdefg abcdefg abcdefg abcdefg abcdefg
abcdefg abcdefg abcdefg abcdefg abcdefg abcdefg abcdefg abcdefg
abcdefg abcdefg abcdefg abcdefg abcdefg abcdefg abcdefg abcdefg
abcdefg abcdefg abcdefg abcdefg abcdefg abcdefg abcdefg abcdefg
```

When you can type abcdefg in perfect rhythm, go on to the second section of the alphabet.

RIGHT HAND   EXERCISE 2.

Extend for h. *Reach for* i *of the* kik,-*combination, then strike home keys* j k l (remembering that you are merely going in the opposite direction on home keys ;lkj). *With your "j" finger reach down and outward to strike* m *of the* jujm-*combination, and inward to the next key* (with the same finger) *and strike* n. *Reach up with the "l" finger to strike* o, *and up with the little finger to strike* p.

Repeat for five lines, or until you have attained perfect rhythm with hijklmnop.

```
hijklmnop hijklmnop hijklmnop hijklmnop hijklmnop hijklmnop
hijklmnop hijklmnop hijklmnop hijklmnop hijklmnop hijklmnop
hijklmnop hijklmnop hijklmnop hijklmnop hijklmnop hijklmnop
hijklmnop hijklmnop hijklmnop hijklmnop hijklmnop hijklmnop
hijklmnop hijklmnop hijklmnop hijklmnop hijklmnop hijklmnop
```

BOTH HANDS   EXERCISE 3.

Starting with the little finger of the left hand, reach up and strike q. *Reach up for* r *of the* frfv-*combination. Strike* s. *Long reach for* t *of the* gtgb-*combination. Now, with the right hand strike* u *of the* jujm-*combination. With the left hand strike* v *of the* frfv-*combination, then (in the* swsx-*combination) reach up for* w *and slip down for* x. *With the right hand you have a long reach for* y *of the* hyhn-*combination. Then back to the left hand for* z *of*

the aqaz-*combination*. This completes the third group: qrstuvwxyz.

For greater facility, remember that R T and V are struck with the same finger. After you have struck R, keep that finger poised to reach T immediately after your S-stroke, and bring it right down to V so that it follows the U-stroke without a break in rhythm.

Also remember that U and Y, the only right-hand strokes in this group, are both struck with the same finger.

Now type five lines of this group as follows:

```
qrstuvwxyz qrstuvwxyz qrstuvwxyz qrstuvwxyz qrstuvwxyz
qrstuvwxyz qrstuvwxyz qrstuvwxyz qrstuvwxyz qrstuvwxyz
qrstuvwxyz qrstuvwxyz qrstuvwxyz qrstuvwxyz qrstuvwxyz
qrstuvwxyz qrstuvwxyz qrstuvwxyz qrstuvwxyz qrstuvwxyz
qrstuvwxyz qrstuvwxyz qrstuvwxyz qrstuvwxyz qrstuvwxyz
```

When you have typed the last group, do five lines as follows:

```
abcdefg hijklmnop qrstuvwxyz abcdefg hijklmnop qrstuvwxyz
abcdefg hijklmnop qrstuvwxyz abcdefg hijklmnop qrstuvwxyz
abcdefg hijklmnop qrstuvwxyz abcdefg hijklmnop qrstuvwxyz
abcdefg hijklmnop qrstuvwxyz abcdefg hijklmnop qrstuvwxyz
abcdefg hijklmnop qrstuvwxyz abcdefg hijklmnop qrstuvwxyz
```

EXERCISE 4.

Now type as many lines as you can, doing the alphabet twice across a line, with no spaces between the sections, thus:

```
abcdefghijklmnopqrstuvwxyz abcdefghijklmnopqrstuvwxyz
abcdefghijklmnopqrstuvwxyz abcdefghijklmnopqrstuvwxyz
abcdefghijklmnopqrstuvwxyz abcdefghijklmnopqrstuvwxyz
```

A NOTE OF INTEREST:

The combination of letters on the upper row of keys (the third from the bottom) form two peculiar "words" when struck in the same order as the *Basic Horizontal Combinations*. They are: qwert and poiuy.

Memorizing these two "words" will give you a further mental guide for your strokes.

The words selected for *Practice Model A* have been chosen for the specific purpose of indicating the proximity of certain letters to each other.

For instance: the word *try* will give you practice in the long and short reach of the index finger in quick succession, and will show you how near *t, r,* and *y* are to each other. The word *man* will acquaint you with the proximity of *m* to *n*. Each word in the first group provides practice for a long and a short reach of the index finger.

In the second group of words you learn how close *x* is to *a* (as in the word *axle*)—and that *c* and *v* are next door neighbors, each remaining within the boundary of its diagonal combination.

Practicing all of the words in this model will give you greater facility and flexibility in a shorter space of time than unselected words.

PRACTICE MODEL

A

Lesson 3

asdfg ;lkjh asdfg ;lkjh asdfg ;lkjh asdfg ;lkjh asdfg ;lkjh
asdfg ;lkjh asdfg ;lkjh asdfg ;lkjh asdfg ;lkjh asdfg ;lkjh
asdfg ;lkjh asdfg ;lkjh asdfg ;lkjh asdfg ;lkjh asdfg ;lkjh
asdfg ;lkjh asdfg ;lkjh asdfg ;lkjh asdfg ;lkjh asdfg ;lkjh
asdfg ;lkjh asdfg ;lkjh asdfg ;lkjh asdfg ;lkjh asdfg ;lkjh

aqaz swsx dedc frfv gtgb ;p;/ lol. kik, jujm hyhn
aqaz swsx dedc frfv gtgb ;p;/ lol. kik, jujm hyhn
aqaz swsx dedc frfv gtgb ;p;/ lol. kik, jujm hyhn
aqaz swsx dedc frfv gtgb ;p;/ lol. kik, jujm hyhn
aqaz swsx dedc frfv gtgb ;p;/ lol. kik, jujm hyhn

abcdefghijklmnopqrstuvwxyz abcdefghijklmnopqrstuvwxyz
abcdefghijklmnopqrstuvwxyz abcdefghijklmnopqrstuvwxyz
abcdefghijklmnopqrstuvwxyz abcdefghijklmnopqrstuvwxyz
abcdefghijklmnopqrstuvwxyz abcdefghijklmnopqrstuvwxyz
abcdefghijklmnopqrstuvwxyz abcdefghijklmnopqrstuvwxyz

try   try   try   try   try   try   try   try   try   try   try   try   try   try   try
you   you   you   you   you   you   you   you   you   you   you   you   you   you   you
jay   jay   jay   jay   jay   jay   jay   jay   jay   jay   jay   jay   jay   jay   jay
man man man man man man man man man man man man man man man

axle axle axle axle axle axle axle axle axle axle axle axle
cave cave cave cave cave cave cave cave cave cave cave cave
axle axle axle axle axle axle axle axle axle axle axle axle
cave cave cave cave cave cave cave cave cave cave cave cave

drive drive drive drive drive drive drive drive drive drive
bevel bevel bevel bevel bevel bevel bevel bevel bevel bevel
drive drive drive drive drive drive drive drive drive drive
bevel bevel bevel bevel bevel bevel bevel bevel bevel bevel

breeze breeze breeze breeze breeze breeze breeze breeze breeze
zephyr zephyr zephyr zephyr zephyr zephyr zephyr zephyr zephyr
breeze breeze breeze breeze breeze breeze breeze breeze breeze
zephyr zephyr zephyr zephyr zephyr zephyr zephyr zephyr zephyr

PRACTICE MODEL

B*

Lesson 3

running running running running running running running running
marking marking marking marking marking marking marking marking
playing playing playing playing playing playing playing playing

mention mention mention mention mention mention mention mention
caption caption caption caption caption caption caption caption
portion portion portion portion portion portion portion portion

capable capable capable capable capable capable capable capable
lovable lovable lovable lovable lovable lovable lovable lovable
notable notable notable notable notable notable notable notable

worked worked worked worked worked worked worked worked worked
mended mended mended mended mended mended mended mended mended
swayed swayed swayed swayed swayed swayed swayed swayed swayed

mainly mainly mainly mainly mainly mainly mainly mainly mainly
sincerely sincerely sincerely sincerely sincerely sincerely
casually casually casually casually casually casually casually
incidentally incidentally incidentally incidentally incidentally

helpful helpful helpful helpful helpful helpful helpful helpful
thankful thankful thankful thankful thankful thankful thankful
wonderful wonderful wonderful wonderful wonderful wonderful

*For those who desire concentrated practice in common word-endings.

LESSON FOUR

CAPITAL LETTERS, PUNCTUATION AND ABBREVIATIONS
AILMENTS AND REMEDIES

Review Drill

1. Type two lines of the *Basic Horizontal Combinations,* thus:

```
asdfg ;lkjh asdfg ;lkjh asdfg ;lkjh asdfg ;lkjh asdfg ;lkjh
asdfg ;lkjh asdfg ;lkjh asdfg ;lkjh asdfg ;lkjh asdfg ;lkjh
```

3. Skip a line and type two lines of the *Basic Diagonal Combinations:*

```
aqaz swsx dedc frfv gtgb ;p;/ lol. kik, jujm hyhn
aqaz swsx dedc frfv gtgb ;p;/ lol. kik, jujm hyhn
```

3. Skip a line and type two lines of the alphabet—two alphabets across each line:

```
abcdefghijklmnopqrstuvwxyz abcdefghijklmnopqrstuvwxyz
abcdefghijklmnopqrstuvwxyz abcdefghijklmnopqrstuvwxyz
```

If you find yourself making the same errors again and again, or if you hesitate repeatedly over a particular stroke, turn to pages 71–72 and select words from the *Alphabetical Word List* containing those letters. Type such word drills until you are absolutely sure of the letter-stroke over which you previously hesitated.

CAPITAL LETTERS

There are two characters on each key. The small characters are the lower-case. The capital letters are the upper-case. To make a capital letter, press down the shift key with the little finger of the opposite hand of the letter to be capitalized.

For a right-hand capital, shift with the little finger of the left hand. For a left-hand capital, shift with the little finger of the right hand. Learn to shift with the little finger without removing the other fingers entirely from their home keys.

Be sure to hold the shift key down until the letter key has been struck and released. If any capital letter does not appear on an even line with the others it is because the shift key was released before the stroke was completed.

By typing each sentence ten times before going on to the next one you automatically become familiar with the letters most frequently used.

For instance: in the first of the quotations which follow, the letter "o" occurs eight times. Typing this sentence ten times means that you will have to strike the "o" eighty times. Having struck the "o" eighty times in a single part of an exercise you'll know the position of that key without having to stop and think about it. The letter "n" occurs six times in this same quotation, and so does the letter "e." Thus "n" and "e" will each be struck sixty times before you go on to the next quotation.

Notice how much faster and how much more skillfully you can type each sentence by the eighth, ninth or tenth repetition!

Now type the quotations. Do not make any haphazard strokes. If you are doubtful about the location of a letter, think of its *Basic Combination* before you make the stroke. DO NOT LOOK at the key.

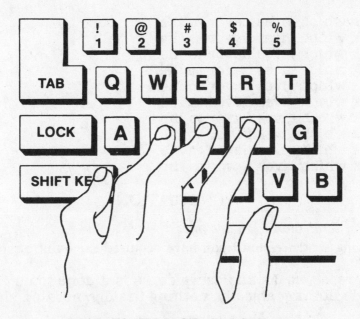

ILLUSTRATES LITTLE FINGER USING SHIFT KEY

No one is so old as to think he cannot live one more year.
No one is so old as to think he cannot live one more year.
No one is so old as to think he cannot live one more year.
No one is so old as to think he cannot live one more year.
No one is so old as to think he cannot live one more year.
No one is so old as to think he cannot live one more year.
No one is so old as to think he cannot live one more year.
No one is so old as to think he cannot live one more year.
No one is so old as to think he cannot live one more year.
No one is so old as to think he cannot live one more year.

A man may know the world without leaving his own home.
A man may know the world without leaving his own home.
A man may know the world without leaving his own home.
A man may know the world without leaving his own home.
A man may know the world without leaving his own home.
A man may know the world without leaving his own home.
A man may know the world without leaving his own home.
A man may know the world without leaving his own home.
A man may know the world without leaving his own home.
A man may know the world without leaving his own home.

The necessity of circumstances proves friends and detects enemies.
The necessity of circumstances proves friends and detects enemies.
The necessity of circumstances proves friends and detects enemies.
The necessity of circumstances proves friends and detects enemies.
The necessity of circumstances proves friends and detects enemies.
The necessity of circumstances proves friends and detects enemies.
The necessity of circumstances proves friends and detects enemies.
The necessity of circumstances proves friends and detects enemies.
The necessity of circumstances proves friends and detects enemies.
The necessity of circumstances proves friends and detects enemies.

It is work which gives flavor to life.
It is work which gives flavor to life.
It is work which gives flavor to life.
It is work which gives flavor to life.
It is work which gives flavor to life.
It is work which gives flavor to life.
It is work which gives flavor to life.
It is work which gives flavor to life.
It is work which gives flavor to life.
It is work which gives flavor to life.

PUNCTUATION

After a comma (,) or a semicolon (;) space once.
Practice the following sentences until you have acquired the habit of spacing properly.

As we are, so we do; and as we do, so is it done to us.
Let us do nothing abjectly, nothing timidly, nothing sluggishly.

After a punctuation mark which ends a sentence—such as a period (.), exclamation point (!) or question-mark (?)—space twice.

When using a period in an abbreviation or after initials of a name, space once.

Space twice after a colon (:) when the following word or sentence begins with a capital.

Type these sentences:

Mr. J. S. Jones arrived this morning. He is from Brooklyn, N. Y.
Mr. Jones is a friend of Mr. Ezra Q. Baxter, Jr.

In abbreviations such as *A.M., P.M., O.K., M.D., Ph.D., and LL.B.*, many authorities prefer not to space after the period. Small-letter abbreviations such as *f.o.b., i.e., e.g.*, etcetera, may also follow this form.

The hyphen (-) (struck with the little finger of the right hand) is used in certain compound words; it is used to divide words at the end of a line when the remainder of the word is carried to the next line, so that a fairly even right-hand margin may be kept. Words divided at the margin should be hyphenated after a *syllable*. Consult a dictionary for proper word-division.

The hyphen, struck twice in succession, represents a dash. You may space before and after the dash, or you may choose to use the dash with no spaces between the words it separates. It is a good policy to stick to one form. Examples of the two forms follow:

She is wearing one of her new hats -- the blue one -- today.
She is wearing one of her new hats--the blue one--today.

The underscore sign (_): The hyphen should not be confused with the underscore sign which is the upper-case character of the numeral "6" key. The underscore sign is used to type unbroken lines across a page and to underline titles, words and passages.

In copy prepared for printing, words are underscored to indicate italics.

Titles and headings: When it is necessary to type an entire word or group of words in capital letters, use the *shift-lock* key, thus:

The title of the book was "SUCCESSFUL BUSINESS LETTERS."

AILMENTS AND REMEDIES

AILMENTS	REMEDIES
Do you sometimes neglect to space between words?	You may be typing so slowly that you forget whether or not you have already spaced before going on with the next word. In that case, let your space-stroke come as a sort of reflex action upon completion of each word—that is: finish the word, then space *instantly* before you begin to think of the next one. If some mark of punctuation follows a word, you will not, of course, space until *after* the punctuation mark. If, accidentally, you should happen to space *before* the mark of punctuation, use the back-space key to return to position for punctuation.
Are you trying to correct errors by striking over them?	Don't. It can become a slovenly habit. In the first place, a strike-over does not correct an error. It merely emphasizes it. Don't be afraid to look your errors in the face. Circle them so you will be able to see where the original fault lies and will know where to exercise caution in the future.
Do your shoulders feel tired?	Then you are too tense. Relax! Your shoulders should be in a relaxed position as you type. It may be that the table is too high, or the chair too low for comfort. Bridge table height is comfortable for most persons, although a sturdier table (one which does not vibrate) is preferable.
Do your fingers and wrists feel somewhat muscle-sore at this point?	Assuming that your posture is correct and that the table and chair are of proper height for avoiding fatigue, this is a perfectly healthy sign. After all, your are using concentrated muscle action different than what your other activities require. Nevertheless, check the position of your hands as you type. You may be guilty of the lazy habit of letting your wrists sag so that your palms are braced against the typewriter as you type! It's much easier on your muscles to keep your wrists up *at all times;* otherwise, it's like trying to drive a car with the brakes on. If an actual physical weakness contributes to muscular fatigue, exercises and practice routine should be rationed.

PRACTICE MODEL

A

Lesson 4

asdfg ;lkjh asdfg ;lkjh asdfg ;lkjh asdfg ;lkjh asdfg ;lkjh
asdfg ;lkjh asdfg ;lkjh asdfg ;lkjh asdfg ;lkjh asdfg ;lkjh

aqaz swsx dedc frfv gtgb ;p;/ lol. kik, jujm hyhn
aqaz swsx dedc frfv gtgb ;p;/ lol. kik, jujm hyhn

abcdefghijklmnopqrstuvwxyz abcdefghijklmnopqrstuvwxyz
abcdefghijklmnopqrstuvwxyz abcdefghijklmnopqrstuvwxyz

No one is so old as to think he cannot live one more year.
No one is so old as to think he cannot live one more year.
No one is so old as to think he cannot live one more year.
No one is so old as to think he cannot live one more year.
No one is so old as to think he cannot live one more year.
No one is so old as to think he cannot live one more year.
No one is so old as to think he cannot live one more year.
No one is so old as to think he cannot live one more year.
No one is so old as to think he cannot live one more year.
No one is so old as to think he cannot live one more year.

It is work which gives flavor to life.
It is work which gives flavor to life.
It is work which gives flavor to life.
It is work which gives flavor to life.
It is work which gives flavor to life.
It is work which gives flavor to life.
It is work which gives flavor to life.
It is work which gives flavor to life.
It is work which gives flavor to life.
It is work which gives flavor to life.

A man may know the world without leaving his own home.
A man may know the world without leaving his own home.
A man may know the world without leaving his own home.
A man may know the world without leaving his own home.
A man may know the world without leaving his own home.
A man may know the world without leaving his own home.
A man may know the world without leaving his own home.
A man may know the world without leaving his own home.
A man may know the world without leaving his own home.
A man may know the world without leaving his own home.

How well are you practicing the rules set forth in this lesson? Are you spacing once after every mark of punctuation within the body of a sentence? Are you spacing twice after each mark of punctuation which completes a sentence? Would you remember to shift for the colon? Type the major rules as an aid to remembering them.

PRACTICE MODEL

B

Lesson 4

After a comma or a semicolon, space once.
After a punctuation mark which ends a sentence, space twice.

When using a period in an abbreviation or after initials of a name, space once.
Space twice after a colon when the following word or sentence begins with a capital letter.

As we are, so we do; and as we do, so is it done to us.
As we are, so we do; and as we do, so is it done to us.
As we are, so we do; and as we do, so is it done to us.
As we are, so we do; and as we do, so is it done to us.

Let us do nothing abjectly, nothing timidly, nothing sluggishly.
Let us do nothing abjectly, nothing timidly, nothing sluggishly.
Let us do nothing abjectly, nothing timidly, nothing sluggishly.
Let us do nothing abjectly, nothing timidly, nothing sluggishly.

Mr. J. S. Jones arrived this morning. He is from Brooklyn, N.Y.
Mr. Jones is a friend of Mr. Ezra Q. Baxter, Jr.

Mrs. Martin J. Browning, sister of Mrs. J. C. Fisher who resides at Marlboro Terrace, is spending a few days in town. Mrs. Browning and Mrs. Fisher are the daughters of the late Mr. and Mrs. Clement B. West of this city.

The following were the first three presidents of the United States: George Washington, John Adams and Thomas Jefferson.

PRACTICE MODEL
C

Lesson 4

Posture is important in developing typing skill.
Posture is important in developing typing skill.
Posture is important in developing typing skill.
Posture is important in developing typing skill.
Posture is important in developing typing skill.

Good light is necessary to prevent eyestrain and fatigue.
Good light is necessary to prevent eyestrain and fatigue.
Good light is necessary to prevent eyestrain and fatigue.
Good light is necessary to prevent eyestrain and fatigue.
Good light is necessary to prevent eyestrain and fatigue.

Copy material should be placed at a good angle to avoid strain.
Copy material should be placed at a good angle to avoid strain.
Copy material should be placed at a good angle to avoid strain.
Copy material should be placed at a good angle to avoid strain.
Copy material should be placed at a good angle to avoid strain.

Practice and determination are additional aids.
Practice and determination are additional aids.
Practice and determination are additional aids.
Practice and determination are additional aids.
Practice and determination are additional aids.

LESSON FIVE

NUMERALS, PUNCTUATION AND SPECIAL CHARACTERS

Review Drill

1. Type two lines of the *Basic Horizontal Combinations*, thus:

> asdfg ;lkjh asdfg ;lkjh asdfg ;lkjh asdfg ;lkjh asdfg ;lkjh
> asdfg ;lkjh asdfg ;lkjh asdfg ;lkjh asdfg ;lkjh asdfg ;lkjh

2. Skip a line and type two lines of the *Basic Diagonal Combinations:*

> aqaz swsx dedc frfv gtgb ;p;/ lol. kik, jujm hyhn
> aqaz swsx dedc frfv gtgb ;p;/ lol. kik, jujm hyhn

3. Skip a line and type two lines of the alphabet—two alphabets across each line:

> abcdefghijklmnopqrstuvwxyz abcdefghijklmnopqrstuvwxyz
> abcdefghijklmnopqrstuvwxyz abcdefghijklmnopqrstuvwxyz

4. Skip a line and type two lines of the following sentences:

> As we are, so we do; and as we do, so is it done to us.
> As we are, so we do; and as we do, so is it done to us.
>
> Let us do nothing abjectly, nothing timidly, nothing sluggishly.
> Let us do nothing abjectly, nothing timidly, nothing sluggishly.
>
> Mr. J. S. Jones arrived this morning. He is from Brooklyn, N. Y.
> Mr. J. S. Jones arrived this morning. He is from Brooklyn, N. Y.
>
> Mr. Jones is a friend of Mr. Ezra Q. Baxter, Jr.
> Mr. Jones is a friend of Mr. Ezra Q. Baxter, Jr.
>
> She is wearing one of her new hats--the blue one--today.
> She is wearing one of her new hats--the blue one--today.

NUMERALS

For the number *one* (1), use the lower-case or small L.

For the numbers of the top row, keep within the same diagonal lines of the *Basic Diagonal Combinations*, using the fingers which control the letters in each numerical combination. The little finger of the left hand is not used for numbers. The first numerical combination of the left hand is sw2—the "2" being struck with the "s" finger.

With the left hand, practice:

> sw2 de3 fr4 gt5 sw2 de3 fr4 gt5 sw2 de3 fr4 gt5 sw2 de3 fr4 gt5

With the right hand, practice:

> hy6 ju7 ki8 lo9 ;p0 hy6 ju7 ki8 lo9 ;p0 hy6 ju7 ki8 lo9 ;p0

Type two lines as follows:

```
sw2 de3 fr4 gt5 hy6 ju7 ki8 lo9 ;p0 1234567890
sw2 de3 fr4 gt5 hy6 ju7 ki8 lo9 ;p0 1234567890
```

Later on, you may of your own accord return to this lesson for further numerical practice. Another important combination we will dwell on today is ;';—because both the apostrophe and the quotation mark are used with great frequency.

To acquire skill in its use, practice the following exercise:

```
;'; ;'; ;'; ;'; ;'; ;'; ;'; ;'; ;'; ;'; ;'; ;'; ;'; ;';
```

Now try ; shift ' for " (quotation mark), ; shift ' for " and repeat across a line thus:

```
;"; ;"; ;"; ;"; ;"; ;"; ;"; ;"; ;"; ;"; ;"; ;"; ;";
```

Type the following sentence five times accurately, and you will have little difficulty remembering the location of the apostrophe in the future:

```
It isn't that I can't or wouldn't; it's just that I haven't time.
It isn't that I can't or wouldn't; it's just that I haven't time.
It isn't that I can't or wouldn't; it's just that I haven't time.
It isn't that I can't or wouldn't; it's just that I haven't time.
It isn't that I can't or wouldn't; it's just that I haven't time.
```

Skill in typewriting is acquired through practice. The more familiar you become with the keyboard, the sooner will you attain speed.

It has already been pointed out in *Lesson Four* that familiarity with the keyboard is best accomplished through repetition. This point must be stressed again and again. Instead of typing a sentence or a paragraph once and going on to new matter, type individual sentences or paragraphs over and over again during practice periods.

You will find that each time you repeat a sentence or paragraph, you automatically pick up a little speed. The important thing to remember is that accuracy should never be sacrificed for speed. If you are accurate, speed will come with proper practice. Do not count on *acquiring* accuracy *later*.

The following sentence which appears in the practice model for this lesson should be included in your supplementary practice:

```
Remember that accuracy should always come before speed.
```

The long sentences which follow should be practiced in this way: Indent five spaces at the beginning of each sentence. Time will be saved if you adjust your tabulator for a five-space indention, and use the tabulator key instead of the space bar to indent. Type the first sentence in single-line spacing at least five times before going on to the next. Skip a line each time you start the sentence, and skip a line before going on to the next sentence—which should be repeated in the same manner.

Do the thing and you have still the power; but they who do not the thing have not the power.

If you would not be forgotten, as soon as you are dead and rotten, either write things worth reading, or do things worth writing.

SPECIAL CHARACTERS

Special characters and symbols above the numerals are obtained by shifting.

@ The *at sign* (@) over numeral 2.
  Example: Jane bought 3 yds. of ribbon @ 12¢. Therefore, she paid 36¢ for 3 yds. of ribbon.

The character over numeral 3 (#) is used to indicate the word *number* when it appears in front of a figure.
  Example: #3207
  When it appears after a figure it indicates *pounds*.
  Example: 92#

$ The character over numeral 4 ($) is the *dollar sign*.
  Example: $9.98 (Note that there is no space between the dollar sign and the figure.)

% The character over numeral 5 (%) is the *percent sign*.
  Example: 25% of $1.00 equals 25¢ or $0.25.

¢ The *cent sign* (¢) over numeral 6 is used after the amount indicated.
  Example: 80¢

& The character over numeral 7 (&) is the *ampersand,* commonly known as the "and sign."
  Example: Smith & Lewis, Inc.
  It is not considered good form to use this sign in place of the word *and* in a sentence.

* The *asterisk* (*) over numeral 8 is used in printing, chiefly as a reference mark.

( ) The characters over numerals 9 and 0 ( ) form *parentheses*.
  Example: H.R.H., is the abbreviation of His (Her) Royal Highness.

All other less frequently used keys at the extreme right side of the keyboard are struck with the little finger of the right hand.

- The *hyphen key* is used to hyphenate words within or between typed lines.

_ The character over the hyphen is the *underscore* (_). It is used for typing a straight line, and indicates italics on matter prepared for printing. Note that it strikes under the typed line, whereas the hyphen strikes on an even line with the letter.
  Example: Underscore strokes ____ ; hyphen strokes ---------.

' The *apostrophe* ('). This symbol is also used for a quotation within a quotation.
  Example: "I saw the man dash through the hall," John explained, "and I called out to him 'What's the hurry?' "

" The character over the apostrophe (") is used for *quotations* and for ditto marks.

/ The "diagonal" key, or *oblique* mark (/) is used in the "care of" sign with "c" and "o" (c/o), though it is considered better form to write out the words "care of"; and it is used to type fractions such as five-sixths (5/6), seven-tenths (7/10), etc.

? The *question mark* (?) is located above the oblique mark.

Note: For making special characters which are not on your keyboard see Lesson Ten, under "Tricks of the Trade."

PRACTICE MODEL

A

Lesson 5

Remember that accuracy should always come before speed.
Remember that accuracy should always come before speed.
Remember that accuracy should always come before speed.
Remember that accuracy should always come before speed.
Remember that accuracy should always come before speed.

Do the thing and you have still the power; but they
who do not the thing have not the power.

Do the thing and you have still the power; but they
who do not the thing have not the power.

Do the thing and you have still the power; but they
who do not the thing have not the power.

If you would not be forgotten, as soon as you are
dead and rotten, either write things worth reading, or
do things worth writing.

If you would not be forgotten, as soon as you are
dead and rotten, either write things worth reading, or
do things worth writing.

If you would not be forgotten, as soon as you are
dead and rotten, either write things worth reading, or
do things worth writing.

Did you type a neat copy of Practice Model A? If your exercises and paragraphs are not spaced apart like those in the model, you are not following instructions carefully. Turn back to page 34 and re-read the instructions for practicing the long sentences.

Your work *can* and *should* look as neat as the printed models. Strict attention to instructions and a little care on your part will enable you to type presentable work even at this early stage.

Form the habit of producing practice pages which you would not be ashamed to show. Pay attention to your margins. You may continue to have an inch margin on each side for all practice work. (For speed tests and letter-writing there will be variations in margins, but for the present, stick to the one-inch margins.) Failure to observe margins will give your work an off-balance appearance. If you are interested enough to take the course in typing, you should be interested enough to bring your best efforts to it. Do you agree? Then let's see how well you can type the next model!

To duplicate the spacing on this model, skip four lines between groups. *The second group will give you trouble unless you keep your eyes on copy.*

PRACTICE MODEL

B

Lesson 5

Doing easily what others find difficult is talent; doing what is impossible for talent is genius.

Doing easily what others find difficult is talent; doing what is impossible for talent is genius.

Doing easily what others find difficult is talent; doing what is impossible for talent is genius.

There is a cropping time in the generations of men, as in the fruits of the field; and sometimes, if the stock be good, there springs up for a time a succession of splendid men; and then comes a period of barrenness.

There is a cropping time in the generations of men, as in the fruits of the field; and sometimes, if the stock be good, there springs up for a time a succession of splendid men; and then comes a period of barrenness.

There is a cropping time in the generations of men, as in the fruits of the field; and sometimes, if the stock be good, there springs up for a time a succession of splendid men; and then comes a period of barrenness.

There is a certain relief in change, even though it be from bad to worse; as I have found in travelling in a stage-coach that it is often a comfort to shift one's position and be bruised in a new place.

There is a certain relief in change, even though it be from bad to worse; as I have found in travelling in a stage-coach that it is often a comfort to shift one's position and be bruised in a new place.

There is a certain relief in change, even though it be from bad to worse; as I have found in travelling in a stage-coach that it is often a comfort to shift one's position and be bruised in a new place.

To type the quotation marks used in this model, shift for the upper-case of the apostrophe key. Do not space between the quotation mark and the word it precedes or follows. There should, however, be two spaces *after* a quotation mark which ends a sentence.

PRACTICE MODEL
C

Lesson 5

```
sw2 de3 fr4 gt5 hy6 ju7 ki8 lo9 ;p0 1234567890
sw2 de3 fr4 gt5 hy6 ju7 ki8 lo9 ;p0 1234567890
```

Although Francis Scott Key wrote the words of "The Star Spangled Banner" in 1814, it was not until March 3, 1931, that the words and music were designated as the national anthem by an Act of Congress, approved by the President.

Ty Cobb, of baseball fame, played right field for Detroit from 1905 to 1926. Christy Mathewson pitched for the New York Nationals from 1900 to 1916.

According to the Queensberry rules, the upper weight limit for professional fighters is as follows: flyweight, 112 pounds; bantamweight, 118; welterweight, 147; middleweight, 160; light heavyweight, 175; heavyweight, over 175 pounds.

As early as the 5th century B.C., parchment was made from the skins of sheep and goats. Was it any wonder that Shakespeare observed, "Is not this a lamentable thing, that of the skin of an innocent lamb should be made parchment; that parchment, being scribbled o'er, should undo a man?"

PRACTICE MODEL

D*

Lesson 5

42356 91807 13857 42356 91807 13857 42356 91807 13857
42356 91807 13857 42356 91807 13857 42356 91807 13857
42356 91807 13857 42356 91807 13857 42356 91807 13857
42356 91807 13857 42356 91807 13857 42356 91807 13857
42356 91807 13857 42356 91807 13857 42356 91807 13857

$123.45 $123.45 $123.45 $123.45 $123.45 $123.45 $123.45
$123.45 $123.45 $123.45 $123.45 $123.45 $123.45 $123.45
$123.45 $123.45 $123.45 $123.45 $123.45 $123.45 $123.45
$123.45 $123.45 $123.45 $123.45 $123.45 $123.45 $123.45
$123.45 $123.45 $123.45 $123.45 $123.45 $123.45 $123.45

27 8/10¢ 27 8/10¢ 27 8/10¢ 27 8/10¢ 27 8/10¢ 27 8/10¢
27 8/10¢ 27 8/10¢ 27 8/10¢ 27 8/10¢ 27 8/10¢ 27 8/10¢
27 8/10¢ 27 8/10¢ 27 8/10¢ 27 8/10¢ 27 8/10¢ 27 8/10¢
27 8/10¢ 27 8/10¢ 27 8/10¢ 27 8/10¢ 27 8/10¢ 27 8/10¢
27 8/10¢ 27 8/10¢ 27 8/10¢ 27 8/10¢ 27 8/10¢ 27 8/10¢

Dec. 5, 1941 Dec. 5, 1941 Dec. 5, 1941 Dec. 5, 1941
Dec. 5, 1941 Dec. 5, 1941 Dec. 5, 1941 Dec. 5, 1941
Dec. 5, 1941 Dec. 5, 1941 Dec. 5, 1941 Dec. 5, 1941
Dec. 5, 1941 Dec. 5, 1941 Dec. 5, 1941 Dec. 5, 1941
Dec. 5, 1941 Dec. 5, 1941 Dec. 5, 1941 Dec. 5, 1941

127,439 127,439 127,439 127,439 127,439 127,439 127,439
127,439 127,439 127,439 127,439 127,439 127,439 127,439
127,439 127,439 127,439 127,439 127,439 127,439 127,439
127,439 127,439 127,439 127,439 127,439 127,439 127,439
127,439 127,439 127,439 127,439 127,439 127,439 127,439

$6850 $6850 $6850 $6850 $6850 $6850 $6850 $6850 $6850 $6850
$6850 $6850 $6850 $6850 $6850 $6850 $6850 $6850 $6850 $6850
$6850 $6850 $6850 $6850 $6850 $6850 $6850 $6850 $6850 $6850
$6850 $6850 $6850 $6850 $6850 $6850 $6850 $6850 $6850 $6850
$6850 $6850 $6850 $6850 $6850 $6850 $6850 $6850 $6850 $6850

*For those who desire concentrated practice in numerals and symbols.

PRACTICE MODEL

E*

Lesson 5

$9\frac{1}{2}$ bu. @ 67¢; $9\frac{1}{2}$ bu. @ 67¢; $9\frac{1}{2}$ bu. @ 67¢; $9\frac{1}{2}$ bu. @ 67¢;
$9\frac{1}{2}$ bu. @ 67¢; $9\frac{1}{2}$ bu. @ 67¢; $9\frac{1}{2}$ bu. @ 67¢; $9\frac{1}{2}$ bu. @ 67¢;
$9\frac{1}{2}$ bu. @ 67¢; $9\frac{1}{2}$ bu. @ 67¢; $9\frac{1}{2}$ bu. @ 67¢; $9\frac{1}{2}$ bu. @ 67¢;
$9\frac{1}{2}$ bu. @ 67¢; $9\frac{1}{2}$ bu. @ 67¢; $9\frac{1}{2}$ bu. @ 67¢; $9\frac{1}{2}$ bu. @ 67¢;
$9\frac{1}{2}$ bu. @ 67¢; $9\frac{1}{2}$ bu. @ 67¢; $9\frac{1}{2}$ bu. @ 67¢; $9\frac{1}{2}$ bu. @ 67¢;

#27 @ $1.35: #27 @ $1.35: #27 @ $1.35: #27 @ $1.35:
#27 @ $1.35: #27 @ $1.35: #27 @ $1.35: #27 @ $1.35:
#27 @ $1.35: #27 @ $1.35: #27 @ $1.35: #27 @ $1.35:
#27 @ $1.35: #27 @ $1.35: #27 @ $1.35: #27 @ $1.35:
#27 @ $1.35: #27 @ $1.35: #27 @ $1.35: #27 @ $1.35:

(58 - 43) (58 - 43) (58 - 43) (58 - 43) (58 - 43)
(58 - 43) (58 - 43) (58 - 43) (58 - 43) (58 - 43)
(58 - 43) (58 - 43) (58 - 43) (58 - 43) (58 - 43)
(58 - 43) (58 - 43) (58 - 43) (58 - 43) (58 - 43)
(58 - 43) (58 - 43) (58 - 43) (58 - 43) (58 - 43)

4% of 102 4% of 102 4% of 102 4% of 102 4% of 102
4% of 102 4% of 102 4% of 102 4% of 102 4% of 102
4% of 102 4% of 102 4% of 102 4% of 102 4% of 102
4% of 102 4% of 102 4% of 102 4% of 102 4% of 102
4% of 102 4% of 102 4% of 102 4% of 102 4% of 102

*For those who desire concentrated practice in numerals and symbols.

LESSON SIX

PARAGRAPH PRACTICE AND ALPHABETIC SENTENCES

Review Drill

Warm up with two lines of the *Basic Diagonal Combinations:*

```
aqaz swsx dedc frfv gtgb ;p;/ lol. kik, jujm hyhn
aqaz swsx dedc frfv gtgb ;p;/ lol. kik, jujm hyhn
```

Type five lines of the alphabet, striving for accuracy, but at the same time trying to increase your speed:

```
abcdefghijklmnopqrstuvwxyz  abcdefghijklmnopqrstuvwxyz
abcdefghijklmnopqrstuvwxyz  abcdefghijklmnopqrstuvwxyz
abcdefghijklmnopqrstuvwxyz  abcdefghijklmnopqrstuvwxyz
abcdefghijklmnopqrstuvwxyz  abcdefghijklmnopqrstuvwxyz
abcdefghijklmnopqrstuvwxyz  abcdefghijklmnopqrstuvwxyz
```

The following sentence contains many of the most frequently used words in our vocabulary. It also contains every letter of the alphabet. After you have typed the paragraph once, draw a circle around each word in which you have made an error, then type correctly a full line of each circled word (see *Practice Model Lesson 6*):

```
        The man said we should do everything in our power to help the
just cause. He made a speech today and we were all there to hear
him. He explained that every citizen was under obligation to his
country. He knew what he was talking about; and we feel it is our
duty to do our part. He requested us to leave our names at the
registration desk. After the talk, we gave our names to the girl
at the desk and vowed that we would make every effort to help the
cause along.
```

When you copy this exercise and similar ones a second and third time, you will find that it becomes easier and is accomplished in less than the time required for the initial effort.

Each of the following sentences contains every letter of the alphabet. As you practice them you will be able to determine which keys you hesitate over repeatedly. Then turn to the word list on pages 71–72, select words containing letters which slow you down, and practice them until you are absolutely certain of the position of the letters which previously caused you to hesitate.

```
Jack Duffy analyzed the quality of good material woven by experts.
The big jumping chef quickly provided an extra dozen white eggs.
Major experimental problems have confronted young quiz trick
wizards.
```

PRACTICE MODEL

Lesson 6

aqaz swsx dedc frfv gtgb ;p;/ lol. kik, jujm hyhn
aqaz swsx dedc frfv gtgb ;p;/ lol. kik, jujm hyhn

abcdefghijklmnopqrstuvwxyz abcdefghijklmnopqrstuvwxyz
abcdefghijklmnopqrstuvwxyz abcdefghijklmnopqrstuvwxyz

      The man said we should do everything in our power to
help the just cause. He made a speech today, and we were
all there to hear him. He esplained that every citizen
was under obligation to his country. He knew what he was
talking about; and we feel it is our dury to do our part.
He requested us to leqve our names at the registration desk.
After the talk, we gave our names to the girl at the desk
and vowed that we would make every effort to help the
cause along.

explained explained explained explained explained explained explained
duty duty duty duty duty duty duty duty duty duty duty duty
leave leave leave leave leave leave leave leave leave leave

      The man said we should do everything in our power to
help the just cause. He made a speech today and we were
all there to hear him. He explained that every citizen
was under obligation to his country. He knew what he was
talking about; and we feel it is our duty to do our part.
He requested us to leave our names at the registration desk.
After the talk, we gave our names to the girl at the desk
and vowed that we would make every effort to help the
cause along.

Jack Duffy analyzed the quality of good material woven by experts.
Jack Duffy analyzed the quality of good material woven by experts.
Jack Duffy analyzed the quality of good material woven by experts.

The big jumping chef quickly provided an extra dozen white eggs.
The big jumping chef quickly provided an extra dozen white eggs.
The big jumping chef quickly provided an extra dozen white eggs.

every every every every every every every every every every
fee fee fee fee fee fee fee fee fee fee fee fee fee fee fee
limiting limiting limiting limiting limiting limiting limiting
invisible invisible invisible invisible invisible invisible

Type each of the following paragraphs in the manner suggested at the beginning of this chapter. Be sure to select words from the list on pages 71–72 if you are having continued difficulty with any particular letter on the keyboard.

THE RACOON

The racoon is a clever little animal who makes his home in the hollow of a large tree, high up from the ground. He is related to the bear. In severe winter weather he hibernates, but during other seasons he sleeps by day and runs around at night. Farmers are often annoyed by the racoon's fondness for young corn, but many people delight in making a pet of the racoon. This little creature is so intelligent and has so much curiosity about anything new that it is interesting and entertaining to have him for a pet.

CURB SERVICE

In the small cities of South America one does not have to send to the store for a container of milk. The milkman walks through the streets with his supply, stopping at each door or window where the customer may see for herself that it is fresh. And how can she doubt it when his supply is kept fresh in the cow which accompanies him?

LESSON SEVEN

SKILL AND SPEED DEVELOPMENT

Part 1

It must again be emphasized that a certain amount of speed comes quite naturally with time and practice, but that the best short-cut to speed in typewriting is by means of repetition-practice. Students who may be inclined to grow weary or bored with repetition of sentences or paragraphs should take into consideration that this method of practice develops skill and speed in much less time than is possible through the practice of typing "something new" all the time.

The typist whose job it is to make a hundred or more copies of a single letter, attains a higher degree of speed than the one who is required to type the same number of letters if each letter is different.

To attain a high speed in typewriting, a definite amount of time should be set aside for practice each day.

The paragraphs in this lesson and the next should be practiced with a view to skill and speed development.

Words are counted in groups of ten and the total number of words appears at the end of each paragraph so that you may come back to this exercise for timed tests later on.

Practice work may be typed in single or double spacing (preferably single), but always have a double space between paragraphs.

There are several things to bear in mind when striving to increase your speed:

1. *Be accurate.* Every conscious error you make slows up your mental process and cuts down your speed.

2. *Keep your eyes on the copy.* Every time you raise your eyes to see if you have made an error, you lose valuable seconds examining the paper in your typewriter and finding your place again on the copy.

3. Do not look up at the end of each line to see if you have reached the margin. *Learn to depend on the bell,* which should ring six or seven spaces before the point at which the right-hand margin is set. If you are in the midst of a long word when the bell rings, hyphenate that word at the first syllable following the sound of the bell. Do not start anything longer than a four-letter word after the bell rings. Occasionally you may find it necessary to add another stroke or two on a line after you have come to the point where the carriage stops. By pressing the margin-release key, the lock is released at the margin and several strokes may be added.

4. Much time may be lost whenever you return the carriage for a new line unless you acquire the habit of throwing the carriage across quickly at the end of every line.

5. It should not be necessary to pause for each capital letter. Reach for the shift, and strike the letter with a quick, easy motion, followed by the next stroke without hesitation.

A HELPFUL FORMULA FOR IMPROVING BUSINESS LETTERS*

A good business letter is <u>clear</u>, <u>concise</u>, <u>correct</u>, <u>complete</u>. These four C's so fully cover the characteristics of a successful letter that they warrant careful examination. (<u>26 words</u>)

Possibly the most common criticism of business letters is that they are not entirely clear. They do not explain exactly what the writer had in mind when he wrote. (<u>29 words</u>)

For example, too many complaint letters do not give clearly the cause of the complaint; too many sales letters do not mention specifically what the reader is to do; too many inquiries do not supply all the details needed; too many other letters have some sort of ambiguity and leave a doubt in the mind of the reader. (<u>58 words</u>)

A clear letter is instantly understandable. Any letter which makes a reader wonder what he ought to do is, to some extent, an unsuccessful letter. The same principle applies to the physical make-up of the letter. If your signature is not legible, it raises a doubt in the mind of the recipient. Have your name typed in. Similarly, if you are writing from the branch office of a national organization, make certain that the reader is directed to answer you at the branch. (<u>84 words</u>)

Make sure that your letter is clear before you mail it. Read it carefully. If it can mean anything other than what you had in mind, remember that the person to whom it is going will probably read the wrong meaning into it. Correct it before you send it out. (<u>50 words</u>)

*Reprinted from *How to Write Successful Business Letters,* by M. M. Swartz (published by Franklin Watts, Inc.) and adapted for use as practice material.

No business letter should be wordy, but there is a[10] difference between being concise and being curt. In their efforts[20] to keep their letters short, some business executives are simply[30] rude. It is entirely possible to make a friendly letter[40] concise. (41 words)

A concise letter tells its story clearly, then ends. It[10] does not ramble on needlessly; it does not repeat the[20] message several times. It has no unnecessary introductions and lingering[30] endings. It is not verbose, neither is it hasty. It[40] is as short as a friendly answer can be. (49 words)

A correct letter is accurate in its statements, and free[10] from mechanical faults. It is not only poor business policy[20] to make statements or claims that are not strictly correct,[30] but it may sometimes lead to legal difficulties. This is[40] especially true in the case of derogatory remarks, which have[50] no place in business. (54 words)

People tend to make incorrect statements when entering a complaint.[10] The normal tendency is to exaggerate the injustice that has[20] been done. This is definitely not good practice. If you[30] have to make a complaint, stick to the exact facts.[40] (40 words)

But whether you are writing a complaint letter or a[10] sales letter or a credit letter -- or any other type[20] of business communication -- you should always stick to the facts.[30] (30 words)

At the same time, make sure that your letter is[10] correct in appearance. That means that it should have no[20] grammatical errors, no misspelled words, no smudges or obvious erasures.[30] Your letter should not be written on a flamboyant letterhead,[40] nor on paper of an offensive color. If you are writing on a personal stationery, let your letter be correct in the sense that it measures up to a decent quality standard. (72 words)

The successful business executive is usually thought of as a quietly dressed, soft-spoken, well-mannered man -- one who is correct in every detail. Whether or not you care to think of yourself as a business executive, remember that your letter will do a better job, as your representative, if it is correct in every sense. (56 words)

The final important failing of most letters is their lack of completeness. They do not give full information. They do not present all the facts that the reader needs for immediate and proper action. (34 words)

To make sure that your letters are complete and specific, go over them carefully and see if you have answered every logical question that might come up. Ask yourself if you would consider the information complete if the letter came to you. (42 words)

An interesting experiment in this connection is to examine the order page of some of the large mail order catalogs. There you will find blanks for your name and address, method of shipment, article number, quantity, size, color, pattern, price, postage, tax, etc. Not all of your letters will be so detailed, of course, but whatever the purpose of your letter, be certain that it gives all the information needed to cover the ground completely. (75 words)

LESSON EIGHT

SKILL AND SPEED DEVELOPMENT

Part 2

Spend as much time as you can in repetition practice of individual paragraphs on pages 37, 42 and 43. Strive for accuracy first of all.

After you have become familiar with these paragraphs through much repetition, time yourself or have someone else time you as a means of determining your speed development.

IF YOU TIME YOURSELF, DO IT THIS WAY:

Place a watch or clock (one which has a second-hand) in easy view. Place a pencil and a slip of paper, or a pad, close at hand. Decide what paragraph or paragraphs you are going to copy. Set copy in position. Set paper and machine in position, ready for typing.

Jot down on the pad the position of the minute and second hands at which you will *start* to type. For instance, if it is seven minutes and five seconds past four o'clock, jot down 7'30", which would stand for seven minutes, thirty seconds—allowing yourself the next 25 seconds in which to jot down the figure and to put your hands immediately in position to begin. (The hour hand may be ignored.)

As soon as the second hand reaches 30", begin to copy. Do not look at the clock again until you have finished copying what you had set out to do.

Immediately on completion, glance at the clock and jot down the position of the second hand before you start to figure the total number of minutes and seconds that were required for the test.

Make a note of your time-record, then repeat the test, striving to complete the next one in less time. Even a few seconds' improvement in time from one test to the next will show you how much can be accomplished through repetitive practice.

ON BEING TIMED BY ANOTHER PERSON:

Give yourself a seven-inch writing line (approximately a half-inch margin on each side). A long writing line reduces the number of carriage returns, so be sure you have the advantage of typing as many words as possible on a line. Don't cheat yourself by using wide margins. This is one time when they are of no value!

A common practice of beginners is to copy from the printed matter, line for line, the exact number of words on the printed line. The printed lines may be only fifty or sixty spaces across the page. If you copy "true to the printed line's end" you are obliged to have more carriage returns per minute than you would have with longer writing lines. So, regardless of the length of the line on the printed page, *keep typing* on one line *until* THE SOUND OF THE BELL warns you when to throw your carriage. THIS IS IMPORTANT. Adhere to this advice and it will pay dividends in accuracy and speed.

Do not attempt anything longer than a one-minute test until you can type 40 words a minute on familiar matter. Do not try time-tests on new copy. Skill and speed develop more readily on material which you have already practiced; skill and speed develop *most rapidly* on one-minute timings. You must acquire a certain amount of skill before you can expect to type at a sustained speed level.

After reaching the 40-word level, try a two-minute test. If you can type 40 words a minute for two minutes, build up your speed on familiar material until you can type 50 words a minute for two minutes. When you reach the 50-word level on two-minute tests, try a five-minute test on familiar matter. Do not attempt a ten-minute test until you have completed the fundamental lessons in this book and have a five-minute sustained speed of between 40 and 50 words per minute.

If your speed tests are less accurate than your usual work, allow yourself more hours of routine practice before attempting additional tests. *Remember that accuracy must never be sacrificed for speed.*

International Typewriter Contest Rules call for a deduction of *ten* words for each error, from the gross number of words typed. Suppose you type 30 words in a one-minute timing and make two errors: your net rate of speed (under those rules) would be calculated as 10 words per minute. If you type 30 words in a one-minute timing and make three errors, your speed rate would be calculated at zero words per minute. Now wouldn't that be wasting a lot of time?

Nevertheless, a much more accurate basis of recording a typist's progress is to jot down the *speed rate* and the *error rate* for each test.

Again suppose that you typed 30 words in a one-minute timing and made two errors. Jot down 30^2. Suppose you typed 30 words in a one-minute timing and made three errors, you would put down 30^3. If you typed the same word rate and made no errors, you would write 30^0.

In a two-minute test, if you type a total of 58 words, divide 58 by 2, and you arrive at 29 w.p.m. (words per minute). If in that two-minute timing you made three errors, divide the number of *errors* by 2 and you have $19\frac{1}{2}$ e.p.m. (errors per minute). In the margin of that effort you would then write $29^{1.5}$.

Keep a daily progress record on which to enter the results of your best timed-effort, putting down your words per minute and your errors per minute in the manner illustrated below.

1-MINUTE TESTS		
DATE	W.P.M.	E.P.M.
Apr. 3	15	1
4	17	0
6	19	0
7	20	1
8	20	0
9	22	1
10	24	2
11	24	0
Apr. 20	33	1
21	33	0
22	35	1
23	37	2
24	40	0
25	42	1
27	42	0

2-MINUTE TESTS		
DATE	W.P.M.	E.P.M.
Apr. 24	29	1.5
25	30	1.
27	31	0.5
28	34	0.
29	35	1.5
30	36	0.

Notice in the illustration that one-minute timings are continued even after attaining the speed from which you graduate to two-minute timings. Keep taking one-minute tests even when you have graduated to five- and ten-minute timings. You will be amazed at how rapidly your skill will develop by the continuance of daily short timings. The long timed-tests may be taken once or twice a week.

See how many zeroes you can record in the E.P.M. column. Reducing your error-rate is a greater achievement than increasing your speed-rate.

Contest rules and the usual school texts calculate words according to the stroke-count. The total number of strokes on timed copy are divided by 5 so that every five strokes may be counted as a word, and 50 strokes are deducted for each error.

Civil Service tests, however, are based on the

actual number of words typed. There is less arithmetic involved in this method and it will be easier for you to calculate your speed by *actual word count.*

The short paragraphs in the following article on job hunting will provide good practice and test material for short timings. Words are counted in groups of ten and the number at the end of each paragraph indicates the total number of words in that particular paragraph. This will enable you to select any one paragraph for speed-building and timing.

For additional short timings you may also go back to page 43—the paragraphs on "The Racoon" and "Curb Service."

Again let me remind you to complete the fundamental lessons in this book before undertaking the longer timed tests. Material is provided in the supplement (page 73) for further skill and speed development. Newspaper editorials and short magazine articles also provide excellent copy.

Each time you start a speed-building exercise, go over the five points you were told to keep in mind in the previous lesson:

1. Be accurate.
2. Keep your eyes on copy.
3. Do not look up to see if you are approaching the margin. *Rely on the bell.*
4. Throw the carriage quickly at end of each line.
5. Shift for capital letters without pausing.

Don't expect to become an *expert* in two or three weeks. The rate at which your speed develops depends upon the amount of time you give to daily practice.

OFFICE WORKER -- DESIRES POSITION

Too often it happens that college graduates with special training and other workers with certain aptitudes spend years of their lives waiting for opportunity to knock instead of going out and knocking at the door of opportunity. (37 words)

They dream of one kind of job but do not know how to go about finding what they want and must therefore make the best of what the Help Wanted columns and the employment agencies have to offer. Even so, the competition may be keen, whether they apply by letter or by personal interview. (54 words)

How much easier it is to invite the job to find you! The Situations Wanted column of a newspaper is a show window through which prospective employers can shop for help -- see at a glance that you are available and decide whether or not to contact you. (47 words)

When you insert an ad of your own you can inform the public that you desire such and such a position -- that is, you may state that you prefer the legal, medical, accounting, publishing, manufacturing or any other field in which you have had previous experience or desire a start. For highly specialized fields, trade and professional journals may be recommended as the best advertising medium. (66 words)

Your ad should be composed with great care, not alone in the economy of words but in stating specific facts as informative as the label on a piece of merchandise. Samples of successful Situation Wanted Ads will be found at the foot of this article. Notice that all but the editor's ad have phone numbers instead of box numbers. No small amount of their success is due to this fact. (70 words)

Office workers should bear in mind that an employer who is looking for someone to type letters for him is not likely to sit down and peck out replies to advertisements requiring written responses. How much easier it is for him to pick up the phone and put in a call! Within five minutes he can have your answers to any and all questions which concern him. You, on the other hand, have an opportunity to learn just what he has to offer, and if it does not appeal to you, no time is wasted in travel and personal interviewing. (100 words)

The suggestion of a phone number does not exclude office workers who do not have a telephone at home. Arrange to use the phone number of a relative, a neighbor or a friend -- but it should be someone who is willing and able to take whatever calls may come while you are out on an interview. The person taking your calls should be instructed to tell the caller that you are expected to return shortly, and to ask for the caller's phone number so that you can contact him immediately upon your return. She should not ask him to phone later on the chance that you might be in. Get his phone number while the getting is good! It is your direction finder; it points to a job which may be of interest to you. It does not hurt to know of as many openings as possible for the more calls you have the better will be your chances of <u>choosing</u> a job. (<u>163 words</u>)

If you make an appointment for a personal interview with the first caller, and if that interview is not successful, phone your "assistant" before starting back. If calls have come in during your absence she can give you the messages; you, in turn, should phone these prospective employers from the neighborhood of your first interview as one or more of them might be in the same vicinity. (<u>67 words</u>)

Contrary to popular belief, Sunday is not an especially good day for office workers to run one-day insertions in the Situations column. Many employers do not want to be bothered about business on their day of rest. A two-day ad, to run on Saturday and Monday, usually brings best results -- for then it is "off with the old and on with the new." (<u>65 words</u>)

LESSON NINE

BUSINESS AND PERSONAL LETTERS*

Style and arrangement, neatness and accuracy are important fundamentals of both business and personal letters. There are various styles to choose from, and interesting arrangements are sometimes achieved by the exercise of individuality on the part of the typist.

In this lesson let us concentrate on the two most popular styles in business letters—*ordinary block style* and *semi-block style* (pages 55 and 56).

Additional styles of letters will be found in this lesson. They are included for the purpose of acquainting you with various features which you should know, to fill a particular need or preference. You do not have to practice these supplementary letters in order to gain a knowledge of their styles. You should, however, study them in order to apply your knowledge at such time as you may be called upon to use the information.

The block style has no indentions in the inside address, the salutation and the body. Every line in these three parts of the letter begins at the left-hand margin.

In the semiblock style, all margins of the inside address and the salutation begin at the margin, but the tabulator is set for uniform indention of paragraphs. Most texts are partial to the practice of indenting letter-paragraphs *five spaces*. There is, however, no blanket rule governing the number of spaces to indent letter-paragraphs. Many firms and individuals prefer indentions of ten or more spaces. The important thing to remember is that all paragraph indentions of the same letter should have an equal number of spaces.

Skip a line between the inside address and the salutation; between the salutation and the body of the letter; between all the paragraphs, so that each one stands out as a separate unit; and between the last line of type (in the main body) and the complimentary closing.

Only the first word of a complimentary closing should be capitalized, as:

Yours very truly,

The signature appears below the complimentary closing. In a business letter it is good form to type the name of the correspondent below the space his signature will occupy. The number of spaces allowed for the signature (usually from 4 to 6 line-spaces) is often a matter of taste or convenience. Allow four spaces for the signature in each of the letters in this lesson.

Typing the name at the bottom of a letter never substitutes for the actual signature. Every letter should be signed with a pen, whether or not the name is repeated in type.

The margins of a letter correspond to the mat of a framed picture. Letters should be properly centered and balanced on the sheet, regardless of the size of the paper used. The usual size of letter or manuscript paper is $8\frac{1}{2}$ x 11 inches. For short letters written on paper of this size, the top and bottom margins must be wider than the margins at the sides. Never start a short letter high up on the sheet and then cut off the excess width from the bottom in the hope of balancing it in that manner. Try to visualize the size of your letter and estimate the amount of space it will occupy on your paper. The appearance of a short letter is often improved by typing it in double-space throughout. If double-spacing is desired, adjust the line-space gauge on your machine.

With time and practice you will gain facility in arrangement. Until then, however, it may be necessary to type a rough draft of each original business letter, from which you can then type a mailable copy. From the draft it will be easier to determine the position of your letter on the page. To save time, "x" out errors in the *draft*

*For personal letters see pages 57, 58 and 59. You may adopt any of them, and will most likely use them all—depending on the size of your stationery or the length of your letters. You will notice that each of the letters reflects something of the personality of the writer. A typed letter can be made to *sound* like a person. Incidentally, take a tip from the college boy's letter on page 59.

instead of stopping to erase, but *never mail a letter with words x'd out*. If errors occur on the letter to be mailed, use an eraser.

The annotations at the lower left-hand corner of Letter No. 1 are the initials of the dictator and of the typist respectively, followed by the word "Enclosure" which refers to the reply envelope mentioned in the letter. The dictator's initials always precede those of the typist.

Letters which are composed and typed by the sender require no identification initials. Annotations, therefore, do not appear in Letter No. 2.

Envelopes should follow the same style of address and punctuation used in the letter to be inserted. The first line of typing usually begins about halfway down the face of the envelope, and several spaces to the left of center.

Be sure to maintain an even stroke so that typed matter will not appear light and dark.

Note: In business letters use the colon after the salutation. In personal letters, either the colon or the comma may be used. The semicolon is never used with the salutation. Remember to shift for the colon.

Make an exact copy of each of the letters in this lesson. If you wish to benefit by the directions given here for setting margin stops, you should know or determine the size of type of your machine. For pica (large) type, the scale is 10 spaces to the inch. For elite (small) type, the scale is 12 spaces to the inch.

If you are in doubt as to the size of type on your machine, measure it in this way: Insert a piece of paper into the machine. Strike the period ten times consecutively. On another line, strike the period twelve times consecutively. With a ruler, measure the dotted lines. If you have ten dots to an inch, your type is pica. If you have twelve dots to an inch, your type is elite.

For both of the letters which follow, insert paper into the machine so that the left edge is at "0" on the front scale. Set Margin Stops according to directions for each letter.

Letter No. 1. Set Margin Stops at 18 and 70, for pica type; at 21 and 83, for elite. Start the date on the 15th line from the top edge of the paper, centered under the letterhead. (The scale for line-spacing is the same for either size type.) After the date has been typed, space down 5 additional lines, and begin the first line of the inside address, flush with the left-hand margin.

JOHN HANCOCK HIGH SCHOOL
CLEVELAND, OHIO

LETTER STYLE
No. 1
Ordinary Block
Style

June 7, 19--

Mr. William H. Marsh
33 Fort Lincoln Avenue
New York City

Dear Mr. Marsh:

I have before me the credentials of Mr. Kenneth T.
Cooper who has applied for a teaching position in
this school.

Your name has been listed as a reference, and I
would appreciate any information you could give
me regarding the personality and ability of Mr.
Cooper.

The opening, which will be available in the Fall,
is for an English teacher, with experience in jour-
nalism, capable of conducting a school newspaper
and stimulating the interest of students in writing
courses.

May I have your frank evaluation of the applicant's
qualifications for a position of this nature? A
stamped, addressed envelope is enclosed for your
reply.

Very truly yours,

Gordon L. Hanson
Principal

GLH:RJ
Enclosure

For Letter No. 2, the tabulator should be set in two places. The first tabulation is for paragraph indention of five spaces, while the second one marks the starting point for all lines of the heading and the closing. This letter-style favors alignment of heading and complimentary closing.

Letter No. 2. For pica type, set Margin Stops at 16 and 70, and the tabulator stops at 21 and 49. For elite type, set Margin Stops at 19 and 84, and the tabulator stops at 24 and 63. Start the heading (the address of the writer, Mr. Marsh) on the 12th line from the top edge of the paper. Space down 6 additional lines from the date and begin the first line of the inside address, flush with the left-hand margin.

```
┌─────────────────┐
│ LETTER STYLE    │
│    No. 2        │
│ Semiblock Style │
└─────────────────┘
```

                                              33 Fort Lincoln Ave.
                                              New York, N. Y.
                                              June 11, 19--

        Mr. Gordon L. Hanson
        Principal
        John Hancock High School
        Cleveland, Ohio

        Dear Mr. Hanson:

             Mr. Kenneth T. Cooper, about whom you inquire,
        was a student in my class of journalism at the State
        University.

             I am glad to recommend him for the position you
        describe. It seems to be an opportunity ideally
        suited to his ability.

             Mr. Cooper's excellent scholastic record, his
        brilliant editorship of the school paper, and his
        splendid leadership at the University, won for him
        the admiration of the entire faculty and the student
        body.

             Mr. Cooper is particularly interested in high
        school journalistic activities. He was instrumental
        in organizing a press association for the high schools
        of his home state, which subsequently established
        scholarships for meritorious students through annual
        contests.

                              Yours very truly,

                              William H. Marsh

Note: Recommended as *easy to read* and *easy to use* guides on letter writing and correct English usage are the following handbooks published by Franklin Watts, Inc.:

How to Write Better Letters and *How to Write Successful Business Letters,* both by M. M. Swartz; *The Practical Handbook of Better English,* by Frank Colby.

MRS. VAUGHN KIRKLAND ★ BABYLON, LONG ISLAND

LETTER STYLE
No. 3
(Personal)
Singled-spaced
indented form

January 3, 19--

Dear Helen,

I'm so sorry I was not able to drive into town with Doris while you were home for Christmas.

Doris tells me she found you, as usual, surrounded by friends; and that she enjoyed every moment of her visit. I wish I could have been there, too, remembering old times, seeing friendly, kindly faces together.

I understand there is a possibility that you may be in town again during the summer. Please let me know when your plans are definite as I should hate to miss seeing you a second time.

Affectionately,

LETTER STYLE
No. 4
(Personal)
Double-spaced
indented form

June
15th
19--

Dear Gladys,

Mother is now well on the road to recovery
and it was safe for me to come home. Her old friend,
Mrs. Forrester (whose husband passed away last winter),
finally decided to come and share Mother's apartment.
They've known each other since college days, and were
as happy as a couple of school girls to be living together again. It's a perfect arrangement!

Here at home I found that our yard, usually
so beautiful this time of year, was a mess! Martin
and I worked for days trying to cut paths around through
the maze of grass which was about knee deep. Help is
unobtainable so we had to do it alone, but we enjoyed
working outdoors for a change. My flowers had just
about given up in despair, so with the exception of a
few potted plants from the florist, we're flowerless
for the first time in years -- and how we miss them!

I hear you've been playing a lot of bridge
lately. I'm afraid my game has gotten a little rusty,
but we're looking forward to resuming our foursomes.
Let me know when you and John can come. Make it soon!

Sincerely,

Note: Letter No. 5. Take a tip from this college boy! Families and personal friends with whom you share much in common will be delighted with your solution to the correspondence problem under pressure of time.

Just be careful not to reveal "confidences" of one person to the others. If you have a "private" message for any of your correspondents of a carbon copy group, add a footnote on the individual copy of the person for whom it is intended.

LETTER STYLE
No. 5
(Personal)
Single-spaced
Block form

Monday

Dear Folks:

What a coincidence! I received letters from all of you today -- one from Norwalk, one from Boston, one from Washington and one from away out in sunny California. Well, the family tree is certainly spreading its branches across the country.

That does have complications: For one thing, all of you ask the same questions and want the same news about my latest achievements (ahem!) at college, and that means writing the same dribble four separate times. It begins to get monotonous. SO -- I says to myself, says I, "Wouldn't it be wonderful if I could write one letter and send it out on a sort of family circuit?" But then I had a better idea -- carbon copies! That's the solution!

If you expect your favorite son and brother to be a leading executive some day, he might as well show a little initiative now. And, believe me -- now is the time when the good old typewriter comes to the aid of this party! You'll all be getting the same news first hand; and, too, each one will know what the others had to write whenever I refer to something particular in any of your letters. Boy, what an idea!

No wonder you couldn't find my pullover sweater, Mother. I blush to confess that I finally found it on a hanger under one of my jackets here. I'm sorry I put you to all that trouble. You'll be glad to know that my memory didn't fail me when it came to my Latin exam. I made a B-plus on that, and an A in political science! I didn't do so well in public speaking, though. Only a C this time. You'll have to give me a few pointers when I come home, Dad.

I hope you girls are going to approve of these 4/c (four copy) letters. All of you asked about my exams, and that question has been answered.

I have no "social affairs" to report, Emily. Mid-term's no time for dates, but don't worry -- I've got a nice little blonde lined up. I told her she looks like you, Grace -- but I was only kidding. She's cute. Ouch!

Tell Bill to let me know more about his new project, Kate. It sounds swell!

Love,

LETTER STYLE
No. 6
(Business)
Indented form

MAITLAND PUBLICATIONS

EMPIRE STATE BUILDING

NEW YORK, N. Y.

21 December 19--

Mr. Geoffrey Holtby
    1056 Carnegie Road
        Cleveland, Ohio

Dear Mr. Holtby:

    In reply to your recent letter concern-
ing a possible story for examination, let me
say that we are somewhat interested. While
we cannot make a definite promise of accept-
ance, we would like to see the story fully
written up.

    We are enclosing a brochure which de-
scribes fully our requirements for the various magazines of MAITLAND PUBLICATIONS.
Please examine this booklet and familiarize
yourself with our stories.

    You may be assured of our careful con-
sideration. I would suggest that you attach
this letter to your manuscript in the event
that you should submit your story.

Sincerely yours,

Thomas Barnett
Fiction Editor

tb/s
Enc.

LETTER STYLE
No. 7
Personal Letter
in Business

Children's Hospital

Mt. Clemens

Michigan

December 17, 19--

Dear Mrs. Cox:

The shipment of books which you
so kindly sent for our library arrived this
morning. We are delighted to have them and
are deeply grateful for your continued interest in the children here.

The selection of titles is wonder-
ful! I shall catalog them immediately for the
sheer joy of witnessing our young patients'
pleasure when the book cart is brought to their
bedsides.

Thank you -- ever so much!

Cordially yours,

_____

Librarian

Mrs. Bertram Cox
805 Highland Avenue
Highland Park, Michigan

KS:GB

LETTER STYLE
No. 8
Two-Page Letter

RESEARCH SERVICE
MEDFORD, MASSACHUSETTS

April 7, 19--

Professor Evan MacDougall
Box 129
Emory University, Georgia

Dear Professor MacDougall:

I was very much interested in what you had to say about that old Georgia hotel register in which the name of H. L. Roosevelt of Charleston, South Carolina appears under date of May 20, 1846. I looked up the Roosevelt genealogy and this is what I found:

Nicholas Roosevelt, father of Henry La Trobe Roosevelt of South Carolina, was born December 7, 1767. He died on July 30, 1854.

He made a boat with a paddle which revolved by means of a tight cord wound around the middle of the axle, and unwound by the reaction of hickory or whalebone springs.

He then became interested in the Schuyler copper mine on the Passaic River in New Jersey, and worked on model of steam engine with Josiah Hornblower.

In 1797 he worked with Robert Livingston and John Stevens in the construction of boats. He believed in his invention of "a vertical wheel" but was over-ruled by Livingston. Livingston later communicated the idea to Robert Fulton who used it.

Because of financial embarrassment Roosevelt could not work independently, but was employed by Robert Fulton.

He attempted to secure patents on his ideas but, for some reason, he failed. His claims were submitted to Roger B. Taney, a famous lawyer, whose opinion was favorable. An early account says: "A suit was about to be begun when the con- sideration of the great expense involved in its prosecution caused the whole matter to be abandoned."

- 1 -

2--Professor MacDougall--Apr. 7, 19--

Henry La Trobe Roosevelt, son of Nicholas,
was born on a river steamer, "New Orleans," on
the Ohio River, on October 30, 1811. He died un-
married at Skaneateles, New York on January 10,
1884.

His mother, the wife of Nicholas, was Lydia
La Trobe, daughter of the engineer-architect of
the National Capitol at Washington -- John Henry
La Trobe.

Going backward from Henry La Trobe Roosevelt, whose
name appears on the register you saw, the genealogy is as
follows:

1. Nicholas (described above)
2. Jacobus, or James -- the ancestor of Theodore Roosevelt.
3. Johannes, or John
4. Nicholas
5. Klaas (or Claes) Martenszen, who came from Holland.

Kindest personal regards, and remember me to
Professor Bravarnic if he is still there.

                              Sincerely yours,

                              Gerald C. Brandt

gob:nw

SAMPLES OF REFERENCE AND "ATTENTION"
LINES IN BUSINESS LETTERS

Alexander Simon, Esq.
1160 Washington Avenue
St. Louis, Missouri 63101
                    In Re: Smith vs. Colitzer
Dear Mr. Simon:

Royalton Credit Jewelry Company
Chicago, Illinois 60607
Gentlemen: Re: Account #37804-L

West End Civic Club
Attention of Mr. B. J. Lansing
371 West End Avenue
Brooklyn, New York 11235

                    Attention: Mr. B. J. Lansing
Gentlemen:
——————————— (or) ———————————
If the letter is intended for Mr. Lansing, personally, and you have no desire to have any other member of the club open it in his absence,
it should be addressed as follow:

Mr. B. J. Lansing
West End Civic Club
371 West End Avenue
Brooklyn, New York 11235

Dear Mr. Lansing:

FORMS OF ADDRESS, SALUTATIONS, AND COMPLIMENTARY CLOSINGS

PERSON	ADDRESS	SALUTATIONS	COMPLIMENTARY CLOSINGS
Ambassador (American)	His Excellency The American Ambassador to Great Britain *or* The Honorable (full name) American Ambassador to Great Britain The American Embassy London, England	Your Excellency: Dear Mr. Ambassador:	Yours respectfully, Very truly yours,
Ambassador (Foreign)	His Excellency The Ambassador of Great Bitain British Embassy Washington, D.C.	Excellency: Your Excellency: Dear Mr. Ambassador:	Yours respectfully,
Archbishop	The Most Reverend (full name) Archbishop of (city)	Most Reverend Sir: Your Excellency:	Respectfully yours,
Bishop (Roman Catholic)	To the Most Reverend (full name) Bishop of (city)	Your Excellency: Dear Sir: Dear Bishop:	Yours respectfully, Yours sincerely,
Cabinet Member	The Honorable, the Secretary of State Washington, D.C.	Sir: Dear Mr. Secretary: *(if a woman)* Madam Secretary:	Very truly yours, Respectfully yours,
Cardinal	His Eminence (full name)	Your Eminence:	Obediently yours, Respectfully yours,
Congressman	The Hon. (full name) House of Representatives Washington, D.C.	Sir: Dear Sir:	Very truly yours, Respectfully yours,
Consul	The American Consul at (city) *or* (full name), Esq. American Consul (city) (country)	Sir: My dear Sir: Dear Mr. (surname):	Yours respectfully, Very truly yours,
Governor	His Excellency The Governor of (state) *or* The Honorable (full name) Governor of (state) (Capital city) (state)	Your Excellency: Sir:	Very truly yours, Respectfully yours,
Lieutenant Governor	The Honorable (full name) Lieutenant Governor of (state) *or* The Lieutenant Governor of (state) (Capital city) (state)	Dear Sir: Dear Lieutenant Governor:	Very truly yours, Respectfully yours,
Judge	Honorable (full name)	Sir: Dear Sir: Dear Judge (surname):	Very truly yours, Respectfully yours,
Lawyer	(full name), Esq. (NOTE: When *Esquire* follows a name, do not write *Mr.* in front of the name.)	Dear Mr. (surname):	Very truly yours, Sincerely yours
Mayor	The Honorable (full name) Mayor of the City of _____ City Hall (city) (state) *or* The Mayor of the City of _____ City Hall (city) (state)	Sir: Dear Sir: Dear Mr. Mayor: Dear Mayor (surname):	Very truly yours, Respectfully yours,

FORMS OF ADDRESS, SALUTATIONS, AND COMPLIMENTARY CLOSINGS *(Continued)*

PERSON	ADDRESS	SALUTATIONS	COMPLIMENTARY CLOSINGS
Minister	The Reverend (full name) *or* Reverend Dr. (full name or surname)	Dear Sir: My dear Sir: Dear Dr. (surname): My dear Dr. (surname):	Yours faithfully, Yours cordially, Yours sincerely, Yours respectfully;
Mother Superior	Reverend Mother Superior (and the initials of her order) *or* Reverend Mother Mary	Dear Reverend Mother: Reverend Mother:	Yours faithfully, Yours respectfully, Yours sincerely,
Nun	Sister Maria Louisa	My dear Sister: Dear Sister:	Yours faithfully, Yours respectfully, Yours sincerely,
Physician	(full name), M.D. (NOTE this example: John L. Smith, M.D.)	Dear Dr. (surname):	Sincerely yours, Very truly yours,
Pope	His Holiness, Pope John Paul II	Most Holy Father: Your Holiness:	Your dutiful son, Your dutiful daughter, Dutifully yours, Respectfully yours,
President	The President The White House Washington, D.C.	Sir: Dear Mr. President: To the President:	Respectfully yours, Faithfully yours, Sincerely yours, Respectfully submitted,
Priest	The Reverend Father (full name)	Dear Father: Dear Father (surname): Dear Reverend Father:	Faithfully yours, Cordially yours, Sincerely yours,
Rabbi	Rabbi (full name) *or* Reverend (full name) *or, if he holds a doctor's degree* Dr. (full name)	Dear Sir: Dear Rabbi (surname): Dear Dr. (surname):	Yours faithfully, Yours cordially, Yours respectfully, Yours sincerely,
Representative	The Hon. (full name) *or* Representative (full name) Assembly Chamber The Capitol (city) (state)	Dear Sir: Dear Representative (surname):	Respectfully yours, Very truly yours,
Senator (United States)	The Hon. (full name) *or* Senator (full name) The United States Senate Washington, D.C.	Dear Senator: Dear Senator (surname):	Respectfully yours, Very truly yours,
Senator (State)	The Hon. (full name) *or* Senator (full name) Senate Chamber The Capitol (city) (state)	Dear Senator: Dear Senator (surname):	Respectfully yours, Very truly yours,
Speaker of the House	The Speaker of the House of Representatives Washington, D.C.	Sir: Dear Mr. Speaker:	Very truly yours, Respectfully yours,

FORMS OF ADDRESS, SALUTATIONS, AND COMPLIMENTARY CLOSINGS *(Continued)*

PERSON	ADDRESS	SALUTATIONS	COMPLIMENTARY CLOSINGS
Supreme Court Justice	The Chief Justice of the United States *or* Chief Justice (surname): Washington, D.C.	Sir: Dear Mr. Chief Justice:	Very truly yours, Respectfully yours,
(Associate)	The Hon. (full name) Justice of the Supreme Court Washington, D. C.	Dear. Mr. Justice: Dear Justice (surname):	Very truly yours, Respectfully yours,
Undersecretary	The Honorable (full name) Undersecretary of State Washington, D.C.	Sir: Dear Sir: Dear Mr. (surname):	Very truly yours, Respectfully yours,
Vice-President	The Honorable, the Vice-President of the United States Washington, D.C. *or* The Vice-President United States Senate Washington, D.C.	Sir: Dear Mr. Vice-President:	Very truly yours, Respectfully yours,
Officers of the Army with grade of Captain or higher	General (full name) Commanding Officer Army of the United States Washington, D.C. *or* Lieutenant Colonel (full name) Commanding Officer (address)	Sir: My dear Sir:	
Army Lieutenant	Lieutenant (full name) (address)	Dear Sir:	
Officers of the Navy with grade of Commander or higher, and officers of the Marines with grade of Captain or higher	The Admiral of the Navy of the United States *or* Admiral (full name) Commanding United States Navy *or* Captain (full name), U.S.N. or U.S.M.C.	Dear Sir: Sir: My dear Captain (surname):	
Lieutenant and Junior Officers in Navy or Marines	Lieutenant (J.G.) (full name) Ensign (full name)	Dear Sir: NOTE: Do not use any designation of rank or title in salutation to Naval Officers below rank of Commander.	

Note: Where a woman is addressed substitute *Madam* for *Sir* and *Miss*, *Mrs.* or *Ms.* for *Mr.*

LESSON TEN

TRICKS OF THE TRADE

HELPFUL HINTS, SPECIAL CHARACTERS

1. CARDS AND LABELS too small to be held in place for typing can be typed with no difficulty in this manner: Take an ordinary sheet of paper. To simplify these instructions take a pencil and write "T" at the top of page. About half way down the page make a fold horizontally across, half an inch deep, so that the open part of fold is upward. Insert the page into the typewriter at the T-end. Roll up past the fold (which may come undone during the rolling but is easily pushed back into shape.) Now the fold forms a "trough" for your card. Insert the card into the fold and roll down to position for typing.

2. CROWDING AND SPREADING: Occasionally it is necessary to fill in a letter which has been left off the end of a word. Position the carriage to the space following the word to be corrected. Press the back-space key only part way, holding it down steadily, and strike the missing letter. Similarly, the back-space key is used for spreading. When a short word must be inserted in place of a longer one, strike the first letter of the word, then space. For the next letter, depress back-spacer slightly and hold steadily in position while striking. Repeat the process until the full word is typed.

```
example              (normal spacing)
example              (crowded spacing)
e x a m p l e        (spread spacing)
```

3. MAKING CORRECTIONS: If you discover a mistake or a typographical error after removing the paper from the typewriter, you should erase it carefully using white-out paper, paint-out liquid, or eraser. Then put your paper back in the typewriter and use the paper release to position the paper at the correct print point. Use the variable linespacer on the left-hand cylinder knob or on your keyboard to align your paper vertically.

Move carriage to extreme right or left to make erasures. See notes on "Care of the Typewriter." Also, hint 5(d).

4. CORRECTION TOOLS: Many typewriters offer a self-correcting feature or special correcting ribbons. Otherwise, various products are available to help you avoid having to retype or make sloppy corrections: paint-out liquids, white-out paper, and special erasers.

5. CHAIN FEEDING: In writing form letters or addressing envelopes you can save time by "chain feeding." Don't attempt this unless you have a highly developed speed. In chain feeding, the next page to be typed is inserted before the previous one is removed. One twirl of the knob ejects the first page and at the same time brings the second one into position for typing. In chain feeding envelopes, prepare a chain of three before you type the first.

6. BACK FEEDING: Legal papers and other documents are usually bound at the top. To make additions or corrections without having to remove the staples and manuscript cover, it is necessary to "back feed." First an ordinary sheet of paper is put into the machine as if for typing. Roll it up until the writing line is about an inch from the top. The bottom of the page to be corrected is then inserted between the blank page and the front of the cylinder. The cylinder knob is then rolled back, drawing the bound sheet into position for making whatever changes are necessary.

7. VERTICAL LINES: Release the variable line-spacer. Turn the knob while you hold a pencil firmly against the page at the point from which the line is to be drawn.

8. CENTERING TITLES AND HEADINGS: Make a tiny crease in the exact center at the top of your page. If you are using manuscript paper, however, and the left edge of the sheet is at "0" on the scale, you don't need the crease. 42 on the scale is the center point for pica type. 50 or 51 is the center point for elite type. Set the carriage at center on what is to be the title line. Count the number of letters and the spaces between the words of the title. Back-space (with the back-spacer key) half the total number of the stroke-count. For instance: If there are 20 strokes (including spaces) in the title, back-space 10 times, and begin to type the title at that point. Center again for the next line, and repeat the process of counting and back-spacing half the number of total strokes to each line.

FOR SPECIAL CHARACTERS WHICH ARE NOT ON THE KEYBOARD

It is possible to buy special print balls or wheels (depending on what sort of typewriter you have) with characters like the Spanish tilde (˜), French accents, mathematical and other technical symbols. On older models, special typebars with these symbols can replace typebars which have the asterisk, fractions, cent sign or any upper or lower case character for which you have little use.

There are typewriters with entirely specialized keyboards for foreign languages and for various trades and professions. There are others with styles of type such as italic, script, etc.

Characters of any standard keyboard can be combined to form numerous symbols which are not on your typewriter. A working knowledge of the function of the variable line-spacer and/or the line-space regulator (which makes it possible to roll the paper the slightest degree above or below the uniform line) will enable you to type the more intricate symbols with precision.

For some symbols it is necessary to use the paper release to position the carriage correctly in order to make these characters and symbols. On page 70 is a list of special characters you can make on your typewriter. Perhaps you can figure out additional ones.

Cedilla	ç	(As in the word *façade*.) Small c and comma. Use back-space key.
Degrees	98°	Use *variable* to roll paper down slightly. Strike small o.
Diaeresis	¨	For the double dot over the vowel (indicating pronunciation in separate syllable, as in the word coöperate) the quotation mark (") is a good substitute. Use back-space key and strike over the letter indicated. No variable spacing necessary.
Division	÷	Colon and hyphen. Use back-space key. (On some typewriters it may be necessary to use *variable* and roll cylinder slightly for best results.)
Equation	=	Hyphen. Back-space and strike again after turning slightly with *variable*. Some new typewriters have a special key for this sign and for the plus (+) sign as well. (See illustration on page 15.)
Greek Letters	φ (Phi)	Small o. Use paper-release to position the carriage and strike *diagonal* (/) through center of o.
	π (Pi)	Hyphen and quotation mark. Use back-space key and *variable*.
	τ (Tau)	Hyphen and apostrophe. Use back-space key and *variable*.
	θ (Theta)	Zero and hyphen. Use back-space key.
Paragraph sign	)(or ¶	Parentheses (in reverse order). *Or:* double diagonal, depressing back-spacer before striking small o. Use *variable*.
Pound sterling	£	Capital L and small f. Use back-spacer.
Prescription	℞	Also to indicate portions of responsive service to be read by congregation. (Valuable in religious book manuscripts.) Back-space only slightly before striking *diagonal*.
Section	§	Small s twice. Use back-spacer and *variable*.
Square root	√	Small 1. Roll paper slightly above uniform line and strike *diagonal*, roll more in same direction and strike underscore sign twice. (Remember that you must shift the 6-key for the *underscore sign*.)
Subscript	H_2O	Use *variable* line-spacer.
Superscript	a^3	Use *variable* line-spacer.
Umlaut	¨	Used in German words or names, as in Müller. Quotation mark over the letter indicated. No *variable* spacing necessary. Simply back-space before striking.
Versicle	℣	To indicate portions of responsive service read by priest or minister. (Used in religious manuscripts.) Back-space to strike *diagonal*.

FOR CONCENTRATED PRACTICE ON CERTAIN LETTER-STROKES

ALPHABETIC WORD LIST

A
alas
salad
data
camera
aggravate
awaken
banana
almanac
animals
capital

B
bubble
webb
bible
ribbed
bib
imbibe
blurb
blubber
booby
bomber

C
click
chick
checked
catch
accent
acquaint
clock
connect
conclude
comic

D
dedicate
deed
indeed
depend
drowned
dreaded
addict
added
darned
ordered

E
element
never
reverberate
belted
elevate
fee
seen
energy
expresses
educate

F
fifth
effort
fortify
afford
effective
fluffy
affair
fanfare
fool
deft

G
gagged
ginger
aggregate
gorge
trigger
laughing
giggle
gauge
haggle
gingham

H
hatched
church
haughty
hunch
humph
hitch
phosphate
height
henchman
headache

I
invisible
limiting
infinite
illicit
ignition
discipline
divinity
diligent
incline
clinic

J
judge
jujitsu
justice
ajar
eject
pajama
rejoice
join
joyous
joke

K
kick
okay
trick
knuckle
knife
kodak
knock
akimbo
eke
sky

L
landlord
lisle
illegible
elemental
allegory
lollipop
lilting
fill
lovely
lulled

M
memory
mimic
mumble
murmur
immediate
management
moonbeam
commissary
moment
emblem

N
none
eminent
annul
anoint
nuisance
anything
nothing
innocent
dependent
indent

O
obey
choose
foot
obsolete
onion
occasion
honor
notorious
cook
portion

P
popcorn
people
purpose
appeal
purple
prepare
pamper
ripple
apple
primp

Q
quest
quake
quilt
plaque
quick
equal
liquid
antique
inquest
aqueduct

R
roar
arrear
careworn
erred
carpenter
furore
further
murder
errand
narrator

S
sense
asserts
assess
assassin
sensation
possess
sissy
schools
satisfy
isolates

T
tempt
retort
retreat
taught
aptitude
tuft
turtle
kettle
rotate
potato

U

ukulele
useful
usury
furious
dubious
beautiful
pursue
urgent
substitute
undue

V

valve
vivid
verb
every
avid
vanity
average
aviation
even
never

W

willow
wreck
worship
awkward
wormwood
owner
allow
window
warp
wigwam

X

xylophone
sixty
expect
index
exam
lexicon
exhume
texture
extract
mixed

Y

young
crayon
eye
psychic
dewy
yellow
buyer
your
dynamic
dryer

Z

zigzag
zipper
quiz
zealous
hazard
horizon
zone
frozen
zinc
lazy

SUPPLEMENTARY MATERIAL

Manuscript Typing

Editors are busy people. To find the best material for their publications it is sometimes necessary for them to read hundreds of manuscripts before selecting the comparatively few which suit their needs. Nothing so reveals an amateur as a manuscript submitted in longhand or in single-spaced typing.

Naturally, a manuscript which is neat and attractive in appearance, and easy on the eyes, is regarded more favorably at the outset. This article tells you how to type a manuscript according to the accepted standard of manuscript typing preferred by the editors who must read them, and by the printers (if you are lucky enough!) who must set them in type.

Double space all lines. Keep paragraphs short and clear for greater reading appeal. Margins should be about an inch and a quarter on the left, and not less than an inch on the right. Indent all paragraphs five spaces.

With the exception of the first and the last sheets, all pages should have the same number of lines of typing—twenty-six, ordinarily.

The most important page of a manuscript, from the point of view of "first impressions," is the first sheet or title page. This is what stares an editor in the face when he picks up a manuscript. If it is neat and attractive, and in accordance with the principles of the accepted form of manuscript typing, the editor does not regard it with the misgivings he might otherwise feel upon being confronted with a manuscript whose appearance indicates that the writer obviously "doesn't know the ropes."

The first page, therefore, should be flawless and show no marks of corrections. Type it a second time if need be, but by all means have a perfect title sheet.

Use a bond paper which will take erasures without smearing or wearing thin the spots where corrections are made. Paint-out liquid may be used to cover an ugly erasure blemish.

In the upper left-hand corner of the title page, an inch from the top, type the name and address of the person submitting the manuscript. In the upper right-hand corner, type the number or approximate number of words the story contains and the conditions of sale, if any—such as, "First Publication Rights Only."[1]

The title should be about four inches from the top of the page. It should be centered and written in capital letters. If the title is short, it is sometimes desirable to space between each letter, triple-space between words and underscore each letter of the title.[2]

Two spaces below the title, type the word, "By," and two spaces below that, type the name of the author exactly as it should appear in print. If the author uses a pen name, the nom-de-plume is typed under the word "By," and the author's real name appears only in the upper left-hand corner with his address. The manuscript starts four or five spaces below the pen name.

Each new chapter of a novel or novelette should be started on a fresh sheet of paper, as if it were the beginning of a new story. The page number appears in the upper right, and the chapter heading begins about three inches below that, properly centered.

To indicate transition—change of scene or passage of time—skip an extra line or two between paragraphs.

A short story or article should, if at all possible, end about half way down the last page.

---

[1]Although music and dramatic works are subject to copyright before publication, it is not possible to copyright books, stories, articles and poems *before* publication. However, if you sell a story to a magazine, you can protect yourself by selling only specific *rights* and not the property itself. By stating conditions of sale you are serving notice to the editors that the property remains yours so that you may sell additional rights such as motion picture, radio, syndicate, etc.

[2]For proper centering of titles see page 69, Hint 8.

Note: For proper arrangement of *bibliographies,* see page 74.

A short line or a few asterisks will indicate the end of a story or chapter. The words, THE END, need not be used except at the termination of a manuscript which is divided into chapters.

A top sheet is sometimes placed over an unbound manuscript. If a top sheet is used, it should have the title and the pen name typed in the same position as this information occupies on the title page.

A stamped, self-addressed, return envelope should be enclosed with your manuscript.

Use only one side of paper throughout.

BIBLIOGRAPHIES

Manuscripts sometimes contain a list of references to indicate the author's sources of information in the preparation of a book or thesis. Sometimes this list is for the convenience of readers who require further study on the subject.

A bibliography may appear either at the beginning or at the end of a manuscript. The list of references are compiled in alphabetical order, giving the name of the author, the title of the book (underscored to indicate italics) the place of publication, the name of publisher and the date of publication.

Here is a short example of a bibliography for a manuscript.

ENGLISH AUTHORS AND
THEIR WORKS
Bibliography

Cunliffe, J. W. English Literature in the Twentieth Century. New York: Macmillan, 1939.

Garnett, Richard, and E. W. Gosse. English Literature. New York: Macmillan, 1935.

Sherman, David E., and Richard Wilcox. Literary England. New York: Random House, 1943–1944.

Supplementary Material for Speed-building

THE HOUSE OF SHAWS
(From Kidnapped)
Robert Louis Stevenson

Out I went into the night. The wind was still[10] moaning in the distance, though never a breath of it[20] came near the house of Shaws. It had fallen blacker[30] than ever; and I was glad to feel along the[40] wall, till I came the length of the stair-tower[50] door at the far end of the unfinished wing. I[60] had got the key into the keyhole and had just[70] turned it, when all upon a sudden, without sound of[80] wind or thunder, the whole sky lighted up with wild[90] fire and went black again. I had to put my[100] hand over my eyes to get back to the colour[110] of the darkness; and indeed I was already half blinded[120] when I stepped into the tower. *(126 words)*

It was so dark inside, it seemed a body could[10] scarce breathe; but I pushed out with foot and hand,[20] and presently struck the wall with the one, and the[30] lowermost round of the stair with the other. The wall,[40] by the touch, was of fine hewn stone; the steps[50] too, though somewhat steep and narrow, were of polished masonwork,[60] and regular and solid underfoot. Minding my uncle's word about[70] the bannisters, I kept close to the tower side, and[80] felt my way in the pitch darkness with a beating[90] heart. *(91 words)*

The house of Shaws stood some five full storeys high,[10] not counting lofts. Well, as I advanced, it seemed to[20] me the stair grew airier and a thought more lightsome;[30] and I was wondering what might be the cause of[40] this change, when a second blink of the summer lightning[50] came and went. If I did not cry out, it[60] was because fear had me by the throat;

and if[70] I did not fall, it was more by Heaven's mercy[80] than my own strength. It was not only that the[90] flash shone in on every side through breaches in the[100] wall, so that I seemed to be clambering aloft upon[110] an open scaffold, but the same passing brightness showed me[120] the steps were of unequal length, and that one of[130] my feet rested that moment within two inches of the[140] well. *(141 words)*

This was the grand stair! I thought; and with the[10] thought, a gust of a kind of angry courage came[20] into my heart. My uncle had sent me here, certainly[30] to run great risks, perhaps to die. I swore I[40] would settle that "perhaps," if I should break my neck[50] for it; got me down upon my hands and knees;[60] and as slowly as a snail, feeling before me every[70] inch, and testing the solidity of every stone, I continued[80] to ascend the stair. The darkness, by contrast with the[90] flash, appeared to have redoubled; nor was that all, for[100] my ears were now troubled and my mind confounded by[110] a great stir of bats in the top part of[120] the tower, and the foul beasts, flying downwards, sometimes beat[130] about my face and body. *(135 words)*

The tower, I should have said, was square; and in[10] every corner the step was made of a great stone[20] of a different shape, to join the flights. Well, I[30] had come close to one of these turns, when, feeling[40] forward as usual, my hand slipped upon an edge and[50] found nothing but emptiness beyond it. The stair had been[60] carried no higher; to set a stranger mounting it in[70] the darkness was to send him straight to his death;[80] and (although, thanks to the lightning and my own precautions,[90] I was safe enough) the mere thought of the peril[100] in which I might have stood, and the dreadful height[110] I might have fallen from, brought out the sweat upon[120] my body and relaxed my joints. *(126 words)*

But I knew what I wanted now, and turned and[10] groped my way down again, with a wonderful anger in[20] my heart. About halfway down, the wind sprang up[30] in a clap and shook the tower, and died again;[40] the rain followed; and before I had reached the ground[50] level it fell in buckets. I put out my head[60] into the storm, and looked along towards the kitchen. The[70] door, which I had shut behind me when I left,[80] now stood open, and shed a little glimmer of light;[90] and I thought I could see a figure standing in[100] the rain, quite still, like a man hearkening. And then[110] there came a blinding flash, which showed me my uncle[120] plainly, just where I had fancied him to stand; and[130] hard upon the heels of it, a great tow-row[140] of thunder. *(142 words)*

Now, whether my uncle thought the crash to be the[10] sound of my fall, or whether he heard in it[20] God's voice denouncing murder, I will leave you to guess.[30] Certain it is, at least, that he was seized on[40] by a kind of panic fear, and that he ran[50] into the house and left the door open behind him.[60] I followed as softly as I could, and, coming unheard[70] into the kitchen, stood and watched him. *(77 words)*

THE FOOTPRINT
(From Robinson Crusoe)
Daniel Defoe

You are to understand that now I had, as I[10] may call it, two plantations in the island: one, my[20] little fortification or tent with the wall about it, under[30] the rock, with the cave behind me, which, by this[40] time, I had enlarged into several apartments or caves, one[50] within another. One of these, which was the driest and[60] largest, and had a door out beyond my wall or[70] fortification, that is to say, beyond where my wall joined[80] to the rock, was all filled up with the large[90] earthen pots, of which I have given an account, and[100] with fourteen or fifteen great baskets, which would hold five[110] or six bushels each, where I laid up my stores[120] of provision, especially my corn, some in the ear, cut[130] off short from the straw, and the other rubbed out[140] with my hand. *(143 words)*

As for my wall, made, as before, with long

stakes[10] or piles, these piles grew all like trees, and were[20] by this time grown so big, and spread so very[30] much, that there was not the least appearance, to anyone's[40] view, of any habitation behind them.   Near this dwelling of[50] mine, but a little farther within the land, and upon[60] lower ground, lay my two pieces of corn land, which[70] I kept duly cultivated and sowed, and which duly yielded[80] me their harvest in its season; and whenever I had[90] occasion for more corn, I had more land adjoining as[100] fit as that.   *(103 words)*

Besides this, I had my country-seat; and I had[10] now a tolerable plantation there also; for, first, I had[20] my little bower, as I called it, which I kept[30] in repair; that is to say, I kept the hedge[40] which encircled it in constantly fitted up to its usual[50] height, the ladder standing always in the inside.   I kept[60] the trees, which at first were no more than my[70] stakes, but were now grown very firm and tall, always[80] cut, so that they might spread, and grow thick, and[90] wild, and make the more agreeable shades, which they did[100] effectually to my mind.   In the middle of this I[110] had my tent always standing, being a piece of a[120] sail spread over poles set up for that purpose, and[130] which never wanted any repair or renewing; and under this[140] I had made me a squab or couch, with the[150] skins of the creatures I had killed, and with other[160] soft things; and a blanket laid on them, such as[170] belonged to our sea-bedding, which I had saved, and[180] a great watch-coat to cover me; and here, whenever[190] I had occasion to be absent from my chief seat,[200] I took up my country habitation.   *(206 words)*

Adjoining to this I had my enclosures for my cattle,[10] that is to say, my goats; and as I had[20] taken an inconceivable deal of pains to fence and enclose[30] this ground, I was anxious to see it kept so[40] entire, lest the goats should break through, that I never[50] left off, till, with infinite labor, I had stuck the[60] outside of the hedge so full of small stakes, and[70] so near to one another, that it was rather a[80] pale than a hedge, and there was scarce room to[90] put a hand

through between them; which afterwards, when those[100] stakes grew, as they did in the next rainy season,[110] made the enclosure strong like a wall—indeed, stronger than[120] any wall. *(122 words)*

This will testify for me that I was not idle,[10] and that I spared no pains to bring to pass[20] whatever appeared necessary for my comfortable support; for I considered[30] the keeping-up a breed of tame creatures thus at[40] my hand would be a living magazine of flesh, milk,[50] butter, and cheese for me as long as I lived[60] in the place, if it were to be forty years;[70] and that keeping them in my reach depended entirely upon[80] my perfecting my enclosures to such a degree that I[90] might be sure of keeping them together; which, by this[100] method, indeed, I so effectually secured that when these little[110] stakes began to grow, I had planted them so very[120] thick that I was forced to pull some of them[130] up again.   *(132 words)*

In this place also I had my grapes growing, which[10] I principally depended on for my winter store of raisins,[20] and which I never failed to preserve very carefully, as[30] the best and most agreeable dainty of my whole diet;[40] and, indeed, they were not only agreeable, but medicinal, wholesome,[50] nourishing, and refreshing to the last degree.   *(57 words)*

As this was also about half-way between my other[10] habitation and the place where I had laid up my[20] boat, I generally stayed and lay here in my way[30] thither: for I used frequently to visit my boat; and[40] I kept all things about or belonging to her in[50] very good order. Sometimes I went out in her to[60] divert myself, but no more hazardous voyages would I go,[70] nor scarce ever above a stone's cast or two from[80] the shore, I was so apprehensive of being hurried out[90] of my knowledge again by the currents or winds, or[100] any other accident.— But now I come to a new[110] scene of my life. *(114 words)*

It happened one day, about noon, going toward my boat,[10] I was exceedingly surprised with the print of a man's[20] naked foot on the shore, which was very plain to[30] be seen in the sand. I stood like one thunderstruck,[40] or as if I had seen an apparition. I listened,[50] I looked round me, but I could hear nothing, nor[60] see anything; I went up to a rising ground, to[70] look farther; I went up the shore and down the[80] shore. But it was all one. I could see no[90] other impression but that one. I went to it again[100] to see if there were any more, and to observe[110] if it might not be my fancy; but there was[120] no room for that, for there was exactly the print[130] of a foot, toes heel, and every part of a[140] foot. How it came thither I knew not, nor could[150] I in the least imagine; but, after innumerable fluttering thoughts,[160] like a man perfectly confused and out of myself, I[170] came home to my fortification, not feeling, as we say,[180] the ground I went on, but terrified to the last[190] degree; looking behind me at every two or three steps,[200] mistaking every bush and tree, and fancying every stump at[210] a distance to be a man. Nor is it possible[220] to describe how many various shapes my affrighted imagination represented[230] things to me in, how many wild ideas were found[240] every moment in my fancy, and what strange unaccountable whimsies[250] came into my thoughts by the way. *(257 words)*

When I came to my castle (for so I think[10] I called it ever after this), I fled into it[20] like one pursued; whether I went over by the ladder,[30] as first contrived, or went in at the hole in[40] the rock, which I had called a door, I cannot[50] remember; for never frightened hare fled to cover or fox[60] to earth with more terror of mind that I to[70] this retreat. *(72 words)*

I slept none that night: the farther I was from[10] the occasion of my fright, the greater my apprehensions were;[20] which is something contrary to the nature of such things,[30] and especially to the usual practice of all creatures in[40] fear; but I was so embarrassed with my own frightful[50] ideas of the thing that I formed nothing but dismal[60] imaginations to myself, even though I was now a great[70] way off it. Sometimes I fancied it must be the[80] Devil, and

reason joined in with me upon this supposition;[90] for how should any other thing in human shape come[100] into the place? Where was the vessel that brought them?[110] What marks were there of any other footsteps? And how[120] was it possible a man should come there? And then[130] to think that Satan should take human shape upon him[140] in such a place, where there could be no manner[150] of occasion for it but to leave the print of[160] his foot behind him, and that even for no purpose[170] too, for he could not be sure I should see[180] it; this was an amusement of the other way. I[190] considered that the Devil might have found out abundance of[200] other ways to have terrified me than this of the[210] single print of a foot; that as I lived quite[220] on the other side of the island, he would never[230] have been so simple as to leave a mark in[240] a place where it was ten thousand to one whether[250] I should ever see it or not, and in the[260] sand too, which the first surge of the sea, upon[270] a high wind, would have defaced entirely; all this seemed[280] inconsistent with the thing itself, and with all the notions[290] we usually entertain of the subtlety of the Devil. *(299 words)*

Abundance of such things as these assisted to argue me[10] out of all apprehensions of its being the Devil; and[20] I presently concluded, then, that it must be some more[30] dangerous creature, viz., that it must be some of the[40] savages of the mainland over against me who had wandered[50] out to sea in their canoes, and, either driven by[60] the currents or by contrary winds, had made the island,[70] and had been on shore, but were gone away again[80] to sea; being as loath, perhaps, to have stayed in[90] this desolate island as I would have been to have[100] had them. *(102 words)*

While these reflections were rolling upon my mind, I was[10] very thankful in my thoughts that I was so happy[20] as not to be thereabouts at that time, or that[30] they did not see my boat, by which they would[40] have concluded that some inhabitants had been in the place,[50] and perhaps have searched farther for me; then terrible thoughts[60] racked my imagination about their having found my boat, and[70] that there were people here; and that if so, I[80] should certainly have them come again in greater numbers, and[90] devour me: that if it should happen so that they[100] should not find me, yet they would find my enclosure,[110] destroy all my corn, and carry away all my flock[120] of tame goats, and I should perish at last for[130] mere want. *(132 words)*

Thus my fear banished all my religious hope, all that[10] former confidence in God, which was founded upon such wonderful[20] experience as I had had of His goodness, as if[30] He that had fed me by miracle hitherto could not[40] preserve, by His power, the provision which He had made[50] for me by His goodness. I reproached myself with my[60] laziness, that would not sow any more corn one year[70] than would just serve me till the next season, as[80] if no accident would intervene to prevent my enjoying the[90] crop that was upon the ground; and this I thought[100] so just a reproof that I resolved for the future[110] to have two or three years' corn beforehand, so that,[120] whatever might come, I might not perish for want of[130] bread. *(131 words)*

SELECTIONS FROM
THE AUTOBIOGRAPHY OF
BENJAMIN FRANKLIN

I have been the more particular in this description of[10] my journey, and shall be so of my first entry[20] into that city, that you may in your mind compare[30] such unlikely beginnings with the figure I have since made[40] there. I was in my working dress, my best clothes[50] being to come round by sea. I was dirty from[60] my journey; my pockets were stuff'd out with shirts and[70] stockings, and I knew no soul nor where to look[80] for lodging. I was fatigued with travelling, rowing, and want[90] of rest, I was very hungry; and my whole stock[100] of cash consisted of a Dutch dollar, and about a[110] shilling in copper. The latter I gave the people of[120] the boat for my passage, who at first re-

fus'd it,[130] on account of my rowing; but I insisted on their[140] taking it. A man being sometimes more generous when he[150] has but a little money than when he has plenty,[160] perhaps thro' fear of being thought to have but little.[170] *(170 words)*

Then I walked up the street, gazing about till near[10] the market-house I met a boy with bread. I[20] had made many a meal on bread, and, inquiring where[30] he got it, I went immediately to the baker's he[40] directed me to, in Second-street, and ask'd for bisket,[50] intending such as we had in Boston; but they, it[60] seems, were not made in Philadelphia. Then I asked for[70] a three-penny loaf, and was told they had none[80] such. So not considering or knowing the difference of money,[90] and the greater cheapness nor the names of his bread,[100] I bad him give me three-penny worth of any[110] sort. He gave me, accordingly, three great puffy rolls. I[120] was surpriz'd at the quantity, but took it, and, having[130] no room in my pockets, walk'd off with a roll[140] under each arm, and eating the other. Thus I went[150] up Market-street as far as Fourth-street, passing by[160] the door of Mr. Read, my future wife's father; when[170] she, standing at the door, saw me, and thought I[180] made, as I certainly did, a most awkward, ridiculous appearance.[190] Then I turned and went down Chestnut-street and part[200] of Walnut-street, eating my roll all the way, and,[210] coming round, found myself again at Market-street wharf, near[220] the boat I came in, to which I went for[230] a draught of the river water; and, being filled with[240] one of my rolls, gave the other two to a[250] woman and her child that came down the river in[260] the boat with us, and were waiting to go farther.[270] *(270 words)*

Thus refreshed, I walked again up the street, which by[10] this time had many clean-dressed people in it, who[20] were all walking the same way. I joined them, and[30] thereby was led into the great meeting-house of the[40] Quakers near the market. I sat down among them, and,[50] after looking round awhile and hearing nothing said, being very[60] drowsy thro' labor and want of rest the preceding night,[70] I fell fast asleep, and continued so till the meeting[80] broke up, when one was kind enough to rouse me.[90] This was, therefore, the first house I was in, or[100] slept in, in Philadelphia.   *(104 words)*

WORD PROCESSORS

Here are some helpful hints about how to use a word processor. Many offices today are equipped with some form of word processor, and it is more than likely that your boss will ask you to use one on the job.

THE ADVANTAGES of word processors are: 1) They allow you to store, revise, correct, and reproduce information, and present it in a variety of layouts and type styles. Computer keyboards also give you access to a wealth of information previously available only in vast libraries. 2) The modern keyboard—found on electronic and newer electric typewriters as well as word processors and microcomputers—is easier to master than manual and older electric keyboards. The new, flatter model provides easier access to keys since there are no steps to climb as in the older models. Numbers and symbols are also more accessible and present fewer reach problems. All told, word processors can help you type faster and correspond or edit much more efficiently.

ADAPTING TO THE TOUCH of a modern keyboard may be a bit difficult at first, especially if you have learned to type on a manual or older electric typewriter.

CARE OF THE WORD PROCESSOR must be exercised with even greater caution than that of the typewriter (as described on page 6); with the reminder that repairs on the word processor tend to be more expensive and even more complicated. We repeat that mechanical adjustments should be left to a competent repair man.

A special note: When using a word processor or electronic typewriter, be particularly careful not to let unoccupied fingers stray carelessly over the keys, or else you will find stray letters adorning the pages of your copy.

OTHER BOOKS OF INTEREST